See Cyprus

Paul Watkins

a complete guide
with road maps,
itineraries and
gazetteer

FORMAT

In memory of
Savvas Patsalides

Acknowledgments

The author would like to express his
appreciation and thanks to all officers of
the Cyprus Tourism Organisation, Public
Information Office and Department of
Antiquities, who assisted in the
preparation of the original material for
this book and in the updating of
information for the revised edition.

Front cover photo: Church of Panagia
Angeloktistos, Kiti. Back cover:
Petra tou Romiou. Front endpapers:
Cypriot shepherd. Back endpapers:
Frescoes in Asinou Church.
Frontispiece: Kolossi Castle

All photographs are by the author with
the following exceptions:
Republic of Cyprus Public Information
Office: 9, 13, 16, 28, 31, 32, 47, 47
86–87 (top), 90–91, 94–95; R. Hodson
25; Peter Larsen 50, 78 (top); Sally
Watkins 63 (top); Camera Press 84.

First published 1972
Revised editions 1981, 1984
© Paul Watkins 1972, 1981, 1984
Published by Format Books
23 Jeffreys Street London NW1

ISBN 0 903372 10 X

Printing by Artes Graficas Grijelmo s.a.
Bilbao

Contents

The island Cyprus is not a large island. From its western extremity, the Akamas peninsula, to the eastern tip of the Karpas (the 'panhandle') it is less than 140 miles, and at its widest point, between Cape Kormakiti in the north and Cape Arnauti in the south, it is less than 60 miles. But in spite of this it has more to offer per square mile than perhaps any other Mediterranean island: more to offer of that total mix of landscape, history and culture that is the substance of this part of the world.

In such a small area, the landscape offers an extraordinary diversity: the result of those cataclysmic earth movements millions of years ago when molten rock broke through the sea-bed to form our islands and continents. The contours of Cyprus bear witness to such an eruption: the central massif of the Troodos rising to over 6,400', the Kyrenia range in the north rising to over 3,300'. The difference in height has created their distinctive features: the Troodos, more exposed to the elements, has lost the sedimentary rock that originally capped it, making it blunter in shape, whereas the lower Kyrenia range has retained its limestone crags that have been more gently eroded, leaving the dramatic peaks and pinnacles that stretch like a barricade along the northern coastline.

Between the two mountain ranges lies the plain of the Mesaoria that originally, as part of the sea, divided the land masses. This plain, which for much of the year has the look of a dry, dusty wasteland, is in fact the most fertile part of the island during the spring months and wherever irrigation has taken a hand.

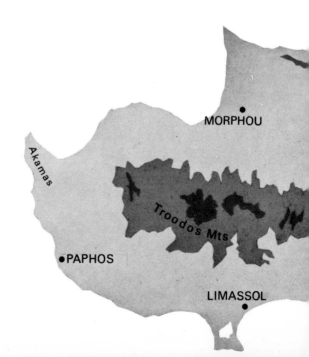

The forests of Cyprus, concentrated in the mountain regions, provide a pleasant contrast to the bareness of the plain. The Troodos, which is almost completely covered by forest, has its own variety of pine, and a unique species of cedar which is found only in certain parts of the Paphos Forest. More common are the beautiful poplars, which grow in the river beds, the eucalyptus, found largely at sea level, and the cypress. In the spring the landscape is transformed by flowers, an unexpected pleasure in this dry corner of the Mediterranean. Their variety in such a small island is astonishing, and although the season is brief — February to April — the contrasts of altitude and climate ensure that many of the more adaptable species bloom in different parts of the island at different times.

Completing the picture of a varied landscape is the coastline of Cyprus. Little of this 480 miles of tumbled rock, white pebble or glistening sand has been spoiled, either by the incursions of industry or the more aggressive tourist development. Wherever you happen to be in Cyprus, you are never more than two hours' drive from the sea and a perfect beach; an opportunity that should not be missed in an island where the sun shines for all but two or three weeks in the year.

If landscape and climate were the only inducements for a visit to Cyprus, then this would be enough to ensure its increasing popularity, particularly for travellers from Northern Europe. But this would be to ignore the fascination of its history, the vitality and friendliness of its people.

The people The island's population of 625,000 includes Greek-Cypriots (77%) Turkish-Cypriots (18%) and smaller minorities. The **Greek-Cypriots**, who look upon themselves as Greeks, have an ancestry that goes back to the Mycenaean settlements of the 14th c. BC. Their contacts with the mother country have been continuous since that time, and are recalled by the alliances with Greece against Persia (5th c. BC), the Hellenistic period (4th–1st c. BC) and the 800 years of Byzantine rule (395–1191 AD) which saw the establishment of the Autocephalous (Greek Orthodox) Church of Cyprus.

The **Turkish-Cypriots**, descendants of the settlers who came to the island during the Turkish occupation (1570–1878) are Moslems and form a separate community in the island, self-administered since the breakdown of the 1960 Constitution and physically divided from the Greeks since the 1974 occupation of the north by the Turkish army. Since 1974 there has been an influx of immigrants to the north from mainland Turkey (not included in the figures above).

Of the other minorities, the **Armenians** and **Maronites** (Syrian Christians) have had the longest association with Cyprus, going back to the Byzantine period when they settled here as independent Christian communities. Apart from the population of the British Sovereign Base Areas, there are a number of British residents.

The people of Cyprus are well-known for their cordial response to visitors. Even in the age of expanding holiday travel they reserve a special welcome for their foreign guests. Their visit is seen as a compliment to the island, and the compliment is always returned with kindness and generosity.

The economy Since the occupation of the northern 40% of the island by the Turkish army in 1974 the Republic of Cyprus has been compelled to make some dramatic adjustments in order to maintain a stable economy. The immediate need was for the rehousing and rehabilitation of 200,000 refugees from the north, who represented about two-fifths of the Greek-Cypriot population. Government aid has provided for the rehousing of the majority of the refugees, and despite the deprivation of its many resources in the north the Republic has been able, as part of its recovery programme, to offer full employment, mainly in agricultural and construction projects.

Agriculture remains the most productive sector of the economy, employing about 35% of the working population and supplying about 65% of her exports. Before 1974 the island's chief export crop was citrus, most of which was grown at the western end of the Kyrenia range and in the Morphou region. Now the emphasis has shifted to the cultivation of field crops, which offer a quick return. Early-growing potatoes are an innovation which has proved particularly popular with the UK: but the future of this market is not assured. Britain has traditionally been Cyprus' best customer, taking up to 75% of her agricultural exports, but with the ending of the preferential agreement on trade in the period following Britain's accession to the EEC, Cyprus is having to compete on unequal terms with her European rivals. These inequalities can only be reduced by Cyprus achieving her own associate status within the EEC, at present under negotiation. In the meantime the island is developing other markets, most impressively with the Arab states. The Lebanese have been particularly active here since the civil war in their own country, and Cypriots working in the Gulf have contributed greatly to foreign earnings.

With no permanent rivers, and an annual rainfall of only 19", **irrigation** has long been Cyprus' most pressing problem. With 60% of the land area cultivated, only 5% is irrigable in the dry summer, and to improve the island's water supply the Government has given priority to dam building and irrigation projects in the Paphos region, which after the loss of the Mesaoria Plain has become the major vegetable and fruit growing region.

Unaffected by the invasion was the island's **wine industry**, centred on the south. The climate and soil of the island are particularly suited to viticulture, which accounts for about a fifth of the total agricultural output. Most of the grape varieties, grown in the Troodos region and in the coastal areas of Limassol and Paphos are native to Cyprus, and two-thirds of her export production of sherries and table wines goes to Britain. The centre of the wine industry is at Limassol, which has four main factories (Keo, Sodap, Etko and Loel). The other industries of Cyprus are closely associated with her home-grown products: textiles and shoes, olive-oil, soap manufacture, soft drinks.

A major source of income for the island before 1974 was from her **mining** products, from the Troodos region. The loss of Mavrovouni and Skouriotissa meant the virtual end of copper mining in Cyprus after 4500 years, but the ore reserves were already nearly exhausted. The chrome, asbestos and gypsum mines continue to be active, however, and a new product, from Mitsero, is gold.

A recent boost to the island's economy was the construction of an oil refinery near Larnaca. More controversial as a source of revenue are the British sovereign base areas, at Dhekelia and Episkopi, which contribute about £30m a year.

Tourism and **light industry** have taken their place after agriculture as the island's biggest earners of foreign currency. Both are labour-intensive, and although the Republic lost 80% of its hotels (in Kyrenia and Famagusta) and the industrial estate of Nicosia, it was able to quickly reactivate these sectors of the economy with the influx of jobless from the north. Tourism has shown a particularly remarkable recovery, and the number of visitors now exceeds pre-1974 figures. The construction boom, assisted by Government tax incentives, continues unabated, with new hotels, apartments, holiday villages and other tourist facilities springing up in the southern resorts. The young Republic has shown a remarkable recovery from adversity, but one can only hope that the price of all this will not be the destruction of the beautiful landscape and peaceful environment which has been the most traditional charm of the island.

Baking bread in a village oven

Cyprus in history

The position of Cyprus in the easternmost corner of the Mediterranean has dictated its history. Like Constantinople it became a point of confrontation between east and west, of the classical and oriental cultures. But its role in the conflict was shaped by its location, 47 miles south of Turkey, 62 miles west of Syria. If Constantinople was a bridge, Cyprus was a stepping-stone. From the east, for the expanding civilizations of Egypt, Assyria and Persia and later the soldiers of Islam; from the west for the Alexandrian generals, the Romans and the Crusader knights en route for the Holy Land. Up to modern times, too, it has served as a stepping-stone, for the empire-builders of Victorian Britain seeking to protect their sea-route to India. With all these comings and goings it is inevitable, perhaps, that only the people who treated Cyprus as a destination (like those early Greek seafarers who came to stay) have had a lasting effect on the island. But what of the Cyprus that existed before the strangers came, before the map was drawn?

Neolithic settlements The origin of the first inhabitants of Cyprus, the Eteo-cypriots, is unknown. Remains of their dwellings have been found in two distinct areas of the island: on the northern side of the Kyrenia range and on the southern side of the Troodos, sited near the perennial streams flowing down from the mountains. The earliest settlement, at Khirokitia (west of Limassol) dates from **5800 BC**. The dwellings uncovered at this site were of the *tholos* type (round, beehive-shaped huts) built of stones and mud from the river-bed. Inside them were found the skeletons of their inhabitants, buried beneath the floor, together with stone vases and implements of bone and obsidian. The latter suggested an early contact with Asia Minor, where this mineral is found. During a transitional period of 2–3000 years stone vessels were replaced by pottery, and the *tholoi* by rectangular dwellings, as at Sotira.

Chalcolithic Period (*c.* 2500–2300 BC) The next development was the discovery of copper in the island, in about 2500 BC. This new metal brought a growth of trade for Cyprus over the next 200 years. There was also a refinement of her pottery, distinguished by the Red Polished and Red-and-Black Ware of Ambelikou. The most dramatic change in the island's development, however, came with the Bronze Age.

Bronze Age (*c.* 2300–1050 BC) Egyptian domination, Greek and Phoenician colonisation The introduction of bronze, which gradually replaced copper, put Cyprus squarely on the map for the rival attentions of the Eastern Mediterranean powers. It was the beginning of a form of colonisation that was to last many centuries, in which the dominant power, without resorting to occupation, was able to assert itself over its smaller neighbour.

Evidence of this is in Egyptian and Hittite tablets of the 15th and 14th c. BC, which record payments of tribute, in the form of copper, by Cyprus (or 'Asy' as it was then known). Throughout the Bronze Age period Cyprus continued as a tributary, mainly under the tutelage of Egypt. But although they controlled the destiny of the island, the overlords made no attempt to populate it. The real colonists were the Greeks and the Phoenicians, who came to the island in the late Bronze Age and established settlements.

The first to arrive were the Greeks, mainly Achaeans from Mycenae. They brought with them a language, religion and way of life that was to become the basis of Greek-Cypriot culture. They also introduced their system of kingship, in which each settlement became a city-state with its own ruler. The most important city-kingdoms founded by the Greeks were those at Salamis, Soli, Marion (Polis), Curium and Paphos (now Palea Paphos). The last-named has special significance, as the centre of the cult of Aphrodite. The Greek goddess of love and beauty, whose legendary birth-place was off the coast nearby, was the island's most popular deity, and the annual pilgrimage to her temple was one of the most celebrated events in the ancient world.

But although Greek influence was paramount, there was at no time any political connection with the Greek state itself. Most of the Greeks who came to Cyprus — particularly after the collapse of the Mycenaean empire in the late 13th c. BC — were either exiles or adventurers, not seeking an expansion of their country abroad but a place in which they could reconstruct their own way of life.

The Phoenicians, who came to the island at the beginning of the 10th c. BC, had more commercial motives. As traders they saw the potential of Cyprus as a staging post on the sea-routes between Greece and the Levant, between Egypt and Anatolia. Their main settlement was at Kition (modern Larnaca), which like the Greek settlements became a city-kingdom.

Iron Age (*c.*1000 BC) **Egyptian and Assyrian Periods (to 546 BC)** For the next three centuries the Phoenicians remained in peaceful competition with the Greeks, under the continuing tutelage of the Egyptians. Then, in 707 BC, the Assyrians under King Sargon II displaced the Egyptians. They forced the submission of the Cypriot kings, both Greek and Phoenician, who were obliged to travel to Babylon with tributes of gold and silver. But although this marked the beginning of 100 years of Assyrian domination, the kingdoms of Cyprus were left to govern themselves — on the condition that they paid tribute and helped the Assyrians in their war against Egypt.

But towards the end of the 7th c. BC the Egyptians reasserted themselves in the Mediterranean, ultimately defeating a combined fleet of Greek-Cypriot and Phoenician vessels in a sea-battle and reclaiming the island. Once more Egypt played the role of absentee landlord, with Salamis, recognised as the supreme kingdom of the island, as her tenant-in-chief.

Despite this feudal situation it was the commencement of a period of great prosperity for the Cypriots, who were by now well established as merchant seafarers. The period was particularly rich in pottery, strikingly oriental in style, as revealed by tomb excavations (Ayia Irini). After their defeat at the hands of the Egyptians, the Cypriots chose their next alliance more carefully. Recognising the growing power of the Persians, who in 546 BC had defeated the armies of Lydia, the Cypriots joined forces with them in a campaign against Egypt. This resulted in the final overthrow of the Egyptians and the ascendancy of the Persians in the Mediterranean, which was to continue until their defeat in the war with Greece.

Persian Period (*c.*546–323 BC) Under the Persians, who finally conquered Egypt in 525 BC, the Cypriot kings kept their sovereignty. But the influence of the new overlords was to upset the political balance of the island. With the support of the Persians, who were their traditional allies, the Phoenician settlers began to deploy from the coast to the interior, where they were to dominate the rich copper centres of Idalion and Tamassos. Kings sympathetic to Persia were appointed to rule over the island's city-kingdoms, and the island's military forces were put at the disposal of the Persian king.

The first Greek-Cypriot rebellion, in 500 BC (which coincided with the revolt of the Ionian islands against Persia) was led by the hero Onesilos, who displaced the pro-Persian king of Salamis and rallied most of the island to his support. Within a year, however, the rebels were defeated by the Persians in a battle near Salamis, and the Persian grip on the island tightened.

The next 50 years, dominated by the war between Greece and Persia, was a trying period for the Greek-Cypriots, who were compelled to join forces with the Persian King Xerxes in his campaigns against Greece. During this period the Greeks, in their efforts to secure a position in the Eastern Mediterranean, made several attempts to invade the island, all unsuccessful. The turning point in the war between Greece and Persia was the naval battle of Salamis (the Greek island, not the Cypriot city) in 480 BC, in which Cyprus committed 150 of her ships on the side of the Persians. The battle ended in a Greek victory and a stalemate in the Mediterranean, resolved finally by a peace treaty between Greece and Persia in 448 BC. This conciliation left Cyprus very much on her own and there followed a long period of struggle for the Greek-Cypriots against the Persians and their Phoenician allies.

The hero of this struggle, and one of the greatest figures in Cypriot history, was Evagoras, the king of Salamis (*c.*435–374 BC). By opening his court to Greek musicians, artists and philosophers, and by promoting the Greek alphabet and coinage, Evagoras did more than any other native Cypriot to advance the Greek culture in the island. Gradually, with the revived support of Athens, he succeeded in displacing the Phoenicians and uniting most of the island under his leadership.

Unfortunately a second treaty between the Greeks and the Persians (386 BC), which reinforced Persian rule over Cyprus, brought about a total Greek withdrawal from the island. The Cypriots, faced alone by the mighty Persian army, retreated to Salamis, which after a lengthy siege fell to the Persians (380 BC).

Even in defeat, Evagoras' power was such that he was able to retain his throne: but a few years later he was assassinated. His triumph, however short-lived, was an example to the Cypriots, but it was not to be repeated. Subsequent revolts were quickly crushed and it took a change in the balance of power in the Mediterranean to secure the island's eventual freedom from Persian rule.

The new empire-builders were the Macedonians, who under the general-ship of Alexander the Great were set on conquest of the east. The Cypriots chose the right moment to change sides. At the Siege of Tyre (332 BC), in which they were engaged to support the Persians with a fleet of 130 ships against the Macedonians, they sent them instead to join the enemy fleet. The result was a decisive victory for Alexander and the eventual overthrow of the Persians. It was the beginning of the mighty empire of Alexander the Great, of which Cyprus now became a part.

Hellenistic Period (323–58 BC) This period of Cypriot history, during which the island was controlled by Alexander's successors, dates from the death of Alexander to the arrival of the Romans. At the outset it seemed that a golden age was promised: the Phoenician influence was virtually ended and Cyprus was at last incorporated in the Greek world. With the rise of Ptolemy, the Alexandrian general who had become Satrap of Egypt, the centre of this world became Alexandria, with Cyprus established as a protectorate.

But the peace and prosperity that the Cypriots craved was not to be. Another of Alexander's generals — the ruler of Syria, Antigonus — made his own bid for power in the island, gaining control of the kingdoms of Amathus, Kition, Lapithos and Kyrenia. The Cypriot king of Salamis, Nicocreon, found himself in alliance with Ptolemy's military Governor, Menelaus, in a war against Antigonus. Although the dissenting kingdoms were ultimately subdued, this was not the end of Antigonus' campaign. In 306 BC he dispatched his son, Demetrius, to Cyprus with a war fleet.

This remarkable young general, who earned the name 'Demetrius the Besieger' met and defeated Menelaus in battle, conquered the city of Salamis after a dramatic siege, and later defeated a reprisal fleet sent by Ptolemy. He seized the throne of Salamis (the royal house of Salamis having already disappeared with the death by suicide of King Nicrocreon) and for 12 years was the sole ruler of the island. Then, after the death of Antigonus and the departure of Demetrius, the island was re-occupied by Ptolemy.

For 250 years his descendants, who all took the name Ptolemy, ruled the island. Under the Ptolemies the independent Cypriot kingdoms disappeared, and Cyprus was divided into four districts with military governors. It was the first time the island had been united, the first time it had been under direct imperial rule. In this peaceful time Cyprus prospered, in close contact with a city that was at the height of its commercial and cultural achievement: Alexandria. But another power was already growing in the Mediterranean: Rome.

Roman Period (58 BC–395 AD) In 58 BC the Romans, already established in the province of Cilicia on the coast of Asia Minor, seized Cyprus as part of their gradual takeover of the Hellenistic world. It later became a province of Rome, ruled by a military governor.

During the Roman occupation of the island, which was to last for 450 years (until the emergence of the Byzantine Empire), Cyprus made the most rapid advances in her history. Roads and harbours, bridges and aqueducts were built by the Roman engineers. Roman architecture survives today in the ruins of temples, palaces and theatres; their art in sculpture and mosaics. Surrounded by the Roman territories of the Eastern Mediterranean, Cyprus enjoyed a long period of peace and security, in which her trade and industry were able to develop unharassed by war or internal strife.

The most important event of the period was the arrival in the island of St Paul on his first missionary journey (45 AD). Accompanied by St Barnabas he travelled across the island from Salamis to Paphos, the Roman capital, and here converted the pro-consul Sergius Paulus to Christianity. On their way the apostles created what was probably the island's first church: a cave in the mountains. This was the home of St Heracleidius, who guided the apostles through the Troodos. Heracleidius, who lived near Tamassos, was ordained by Paul as the island's first bishop.

As the first port-of-call in Paul's great journey, Cyprus has a special significance in the early Christian Church. The other event that was to prove of great importance to the foundation of the independent Cypriot Church was the later

Temple of Apollo, Curium

martyrdom here of St Barnabas, who was a native of Cyprus. The missionary saint was martyred by the Jews, who were established in some strength in the island, having fled here to escape the persecution of the Romans in Palestine.

The rise of Christianity in Cyprus met with continuing resistance by the Jews, and in 117 AD there was a terrible massacre in Salamis, in which most of the Gentile population lost their lives. The Romans, who had already put down Jewish insurrections in Palestine and elsewhere, immediately expelled all Jews from Cyprus. By 313 AD, when the Emperor Constantine officially recognised Christianity, most of Cyprus had become Christian, and was later represented by three bishops at the first Ecumenical Council, summoned at Nicaea.

A further notable event in the history of the Cypriot Church was the visit of the Empress Helena, mother of Constantine, in 324 AD. The Empress, returning to Rome after a journey to Jerusalem, brought with her relics of the True Cross, a fragment of which was to be enshrined in the monastery founded by her on Stavrovouni. It was a symbol of the new faith, which now largely united the Roman world that stretched from the Atlantic to the Euphrates. But ultimately Christianity could not prevent the break-up of an empire that had become too vast to govern itself effectively, or to withstand the barbarian pressure on its borders.

Byzantine Period (395–1191) In 395 AD the Roman Empire was divided into two parts, with an eastern capital at Byzantium (later Constantinople) which was to take Cyprus back into the orbit of the Greek world. But it was not only political events that altered the destiny of Cyprus in the 4th c. AD. Earthquakes, which had been common throughout the Roman period, were particularly severe at this time. The cities of Paphos and Salamis were almost completely destroyed. When Salamis was rebuilt in 350 AD it was renamed Constantia, in honour of the Emperor. It was, however, never to recover its former splendour.

As part of the Eastern Byzantine Empire Cyprus was ruled, in both its religious and secular affairs, by Antioch in Syria, the capital of the diocese to which it now belonged. It was not a situation which the Church of Cyprus, with its own special history, could happily accept. A campaign for autonomy was mounted which came to a climax with the discovery, in 477 AD, of the remains of St Barnabas, the missionary martyr, in a rock tomb near Salamis. A copy of St Matthew's Gospel, found in the tomb, was presented to the Byzantine Emperor by the Cypriot Archbishop Anthemios, and the discovery was accepted as proof of the foundation of the Church of Cyprus by the apostle Paul. The autonomy, or autocephaly of the Church was recognised, and the Archbishop, who became its supreme head, was accorded special privileges which survive to this day.

A long period of peace followed, in which the Byzantine Empire, cemented by the strengthening of Christianity, remained unchallenged. Then, in the middle of the 7th c., a new faith emerged in the east, propelling its forces across the Holy Land: Islam.

For three centuries (648–965) Cyprus was subjected to a series of Arab raids, launched from the Syrian coast. The great city of Constantia was destroyed, never to be rebuilt, and most of the island's churches ransacked and torn down. It was not until the late 10th c. that Cyprus was freed from the threat of Arab invasions by the Emperor Nicephorus Phocas, who defeated the Saracens and ushered in a further period of peace and security in which the Church held sway over the life of the island. It was the start of the Golden Age of the Byzantine Empire, in which Cyprus, a primary refuge of Christianity during the continuing Arab expansion in the Holy Land, participated to the full.

Cypriot Christian art reached its apogee in the architecture and decoration of the new churches and monasteries that sprang up throughout the island, leaving as its most superb achievement the wall paintings of the tiny churches, built largely by private donors, that are to be found tucked away in remote villages. Another change was in the development of the new towns, replacing those destroyed by the Arab invaders. Most important were Ammochostos (later Famagusta) which replaced Constantia, Larnaca which replaced Kition, Lemesos (later Limassol) which replaced Amathus and Lefkosia (Nicosia) which was built on the site of the ancient settlement of Ledra. Also built in this period were the great castles, part of the island's defences against further possible Arab invasions, which were sited at various strategic points on the coast and on the Kyrenia mountain range. The sense of security which had created the new towns was thereby reinforced.

In the 11th c., however, that security began to look increasingly uncertain. The Seljuk Turks, precursors of the Ottomans, had taken over the banner of Islam – and the city of Jerusalem – from the Arabs, and were threatening the Byzantine Empire. For the moment, the barrier of the Mediterranean kept the Turks out of Cyprus – but they were to be the indirect cause of the next change in the course of Cypriot history.

The First Crusade, mounted in 1095, was led largely by the knights and princes of Western Europe, spurred on by

Wall painting in Asinou Church

the Pope. There had already been the Great Schism between the Roman Catholic and Greek Orthodox Churches (1054) and now a situation was developing in which the rival Churches were in direct confrontation, with the Crusader armies marching via Constantinople to the Holy Land. With their capture of Jerusalem from the Turks (1099) and the establishment of Crusader states from Antioch in Syria to the Egyptian frontier, the Frankish knights and their followers became a strong, albeit temporary, power in the Eastern Mediterranean. The Byzantine Empire, largely overrun by the Turks, was at the same time rapidly declining, and its influence over Cyprus, one of its last territories, declined with it.

In 1184 a rebel Byzantine prince, Isaac Comnenus, proclaimed himself Emperor of Cyprus. His despotic rule, which lasted for seven years, was challenged by Constantinople but only terminated by the King of England, Richard the Lionheart, who landed on the island on his way to join the Third Crusade.

Richard I and the Templars (1191)

Isaac's forces were quickly routed by the English king, and the despot pursued into the mountains. Richard, meanwhile, married Berengaria, the French princess who had accompanied him on his voyage, in Limassol castle. After the capture and deportation of Isaac, Richard himself left the island for Acre in the Holy Land. His devotion to the Crusade was greater than any interest he might have had in Cyprus, and within a year of his conquest he sold the island to his fellow-Crusaders, the Knights Templar, to raise funds for his army. The conditions of the sale, however, made the position of the Templars as rulers immediately untenable: having paid four-tenths of the sum as a down-payment they had to raise the remainder by taxation. The Cypriots rebelled and the Knights had to crush them ruthlessly to save their own lives.

Realising that they would be unable to hold the island, the Templars asked Richard to let them return Cyprus to his administration. To this Richard agreed, but carefully omitted to repay the Templar's down payment. In light of this, it was appropriate that the English king should then resell the island to another Crusader ally, Guy de Lusignan, for the same price as he had offered it to the Templars.

Lusignan Period (1192–1489) Guy de Lusignan was a French noble who had been the last King of Jerusalem (at that time one of the Crusader states) before the city had fallen to the overwhelming forces of the Mohammedan leader Saladin (1187). After his defeat in the Holy Land, Cyprus was a consolation prize, and as Lord of Cyprus he established here a patronage and a feudal system of rule that recreated the Kingdom of Jerusalem. Other Crusaders, such as the Knights of St John (Hospitallers) at Limassol, were granted certain parts of the island to administer on the same basis. Guy's successor, his brother Amaury, assumed the title King of Cyprus and later, to identify with their lost territory in the Holy Land, King of Jerusalem.

Under the Lusignan kings, Cyprus entered the most spectacular period of its history. Palaces, churches and fortifications were built, and the crumbling Byzantine castles refortified. Nicosia and Famagusta became the chief cities of the island, with magnificent cathedrals, built in the French Gothic style, that survive to this day. After the fall of Acre (1291), the last Christian stronghold in the Holy Land, Famagusta became particularly prosperous. In its new position as the easternmost outpost of Christendom, Cyprus became the centre of trade in the Eastern Mediterranean, with the port of Famagusta as the meeting-place for rich merchants from all over the world.

But the prosperity of the island was not shared by its inhabitants, the Greek-Cypriot people, who were more alienated by the Lusignans' Catholic, French-speaking dynasty than they had been by any previous foreign power. It was not merely the serfdom that was imposed on them by the Latin rulers but the discrimination against their Church, which became particularly rigorous after the Papal Bull of 1260, which made the Orthodox Church subject to the Church of Rome, and Catholicism the official religion of Cyprus. The Archbishopric, which had given the people their spiritual guidance for more than eight centuries, was suppressed. Rebellion against the Crusader knights, with all their military skills, was impossible, and the Cypriots, as so often in their history, were forced to endure and to bide their time until the next change of current in the Mediterranean.

The shift of power, when it occurred, came not from outside the island but from within. The merchant princes of Cyprus, the Genoese and Venetians, had long been rivals, vying for control not only of the island's trade but of the port of Famagusta. The conflict was brought to a head in 1372 by an incident at the coronation of a Lusignan king, Peter II, in Famagusta. A dispute as to whether a Genoese or a Venetian should have the privilege of holding the right-hand rein of the king's horse as he rode out of the cathedral ended in a riot, in which many Genoese were killed and their houses plundered.

The Genoese reacted violently. In 1373 a reprisal fleet was dispatched from Genoa and the island was invaded. All the major towns were overrun, the king captured and his mother, Eleanor of Aragon, besieged in Kyrenia Castle. Aided by their Bulgarian mercenaries the Franks retaliated and for more than a year the island was at war, without any clear advantage to either side. In the end a peace settlement was concluded, in which the Lusignan king was restored to his throne and Famagusta ceded to the Genoese.

Lusignan rule, already severely undermined, was to suffer greater threats in the 15th c. This time it was the Egyptian Mamelukes, and history was to repeat itself with singular cruelty. The Mamelukes, originally a group of Circassian slaves who had seized power in Egypt in 1254 and joined the Turks in their struggle against the Christians, had long had greedy eyes on Cyprus. In 1424–25 they attacked and plundered Limassol and Larnaca, and the following year landed a larger force and marched on Nicosia. The king, Janus, set out with an army to meet them, but was defeated by the Mamelukes at Khirokitia and taken prisoner. The Mamelukes, continuing their march, took Nicosia and pillaged the city of its treasures, which they carried back with them to Alexandria — together with the king. Janus was later released, after the payment of a ransom and the agreement that Cyprus should recognise the suzerainty of the Sultan. For the Cypriots, the clock was put back two thousand years: once more they were paying tribute to a foreign overlord, Egypt. The power of the Lusignan dynasty was eroded forever and there followed a series of feuds in which claimants supported by the two rival Churches — Catholic and Orthodox — engaged in a struggle for the throne.

After the last Lusignan king, Jacques, had wrested Famagusta from the Genoese and taken a Venetian bride, Caterina Cornaro, the political scales tipped in favour of Venice. When both Jacques and his infant son had died in mysterious circumstances, leaving Queen Caterina on the throne of Cyprus, the way was clear for a Venetian takeover.

Venetian Period (1489–1571) In 1489 the Venetians persuaded Caterina to return to Italy, appointed a military governor for the island, and concluded an alliance with Egypt. For a city republic like Venice, whose wealth had been founded on trade, Cyprus provided an important strategic outpost from which to protect its sea-routes. The Venetians' primary concern became the military defence of the island, and to this end they greatly strengthened the fortifications of Kyrenia and Famagusta and built a circular wall, with moat and bastions, around the capital city of Nicosia. The introduction of gunpowder and siege cannon called for a new type of fortification, with thick walls and squat, rounded towers. In the construction of these new fortress-cities many fine buildings of the Lusignan period were destroyed, and the old Byzantine castles which the Lusignans had fortified — St Hilarion, Buffavento and Kantara — were dismantled.

While the new masters built their island stronghold, the people continued to live in serfdom and poverty, the natural resources of the island being largely neglected by the Venetians. The enemy, looming large on the horizon, was the Ottoman Turks. With their conquest of Constantinople, last bastion of the Byzantine Empire, in the north, and the submission of the Egyptian Mamelukes in the south, the Turks now enclosed Cyprus and needed only to capture the island to gain control of the Eastern Mediterranean.

In 1570 Sultan Selim II demanded the cession of Cyprus to Turkey, claiming that its conquest by Egypt in the previous century made it legitimately a part of the Sultanate. When Venice refused the demand, the Turks declared war on Cyprus. The first invasion fleet, which arrived at Larnaca, met with no resistance from the Cypriot people, who were only too keen to see the overthrow of the

Venetians. The only opposition was presented by the three Venetian strongholds, at Nicosia, Kyrenia and Famagusta.

The first to fall was Nicosia, after a siege of six weeks in which the newly-constructed walls were finally breached by the determined onslaughts of the Turks. When news of the capture of Nicosia and the massacre of its inhabitants reached Kyrenia the garrison there, which was undermanned and lacked outside support, quickly surrendered.

There remained only the mighty city and port of Famagusta, as the last outpost of Christianity in the East, to defy the Turkish conquerors. The Turkish commander, Lala Mustafa Pasha, held back for several months, awaiting reinforcements. Then, in the spring of 1571, he launched his attack on the city.

The odds were against the Venetians from the start. Against a Turkish force of more than 200,000 they could muster only 8,000 defenders. But for five months they held out, the massive walls of the city withstanding a prolonged close-range bombardment in which something like 100,000 cannon-balls fell on the city. In the end it was the loss of defenders, the shortage of food and ammunition and the failure of help from Venice or elsewhere that forced the Venetian commander, Bragadino, to surrender.

After their astonishing display of fortitude Mustafa Pasha was prepared to treat his Venetian captives honourably; but on learning that Bragadino had executed a number of Turks captured during the siege his attitude changed. A wholesale slaughter of Christians commenced, and Bragadino, after being subjected to two weeks of torture, was flayed alive in the public square and his skin stuffed and displayed as a symbol of Turkish triumph and Venetian perfidy.

On hearing news of the capture of Famagusta, and this spectacular personal atrocity, the European powers took belated action. In October 1571 a fleet assembled by the Holy League of Spain, Genoa and Venice defeated the Turks in the great sea battle of Lepanto, at the entrance to the Gulf of Corinth. But although it was a decisive victory for Christendom it had little effect on the continuing expansion of the Ottoman Empire or the future of Cyprus which was now abandoned, for more than three centuries, to Turkish rule.

Turkish Period (1571–1878) Apart from their hatred of the Venetians, the main reason that the Cypriots had welcomed the arrival of the Turks was their knowledge that the Ottomans – unlike the Latin rulers – recognised the Greek Orthodox Church. One of the first actions of the Turks, in fact, was to restore the Archbishopric. They also abolished the feudal system and freed the serfs. But it did not, in the long run, make the lot of the Cypriots any happier. The religious tolerance of the Turks had a very practical motivation. By acknowledging the authority of the church leaders they were able to use them as an extension of their administration, for the purpose of collecting taxes. Religious freedom was a privilege the Cypriots had to pay for, along with other privileges such as exemption from military service. Most of this tax money went directly to Istanbul, and the Cypriots had little benefit from it in the way of development within the island. Evidence of this is in the paucity of non-domestic Turkish building to be seen in Cyprus, after 300 years of occupation. Many of the mosques are converted Latin churches, and most of the other large buildings that survive from the period are military.

Like many of the occupying powers before them, the Turks were on the defensive. In 1821 the revolution against Turkish rule in Greece found an emotional response in the Greek-Cypriots: to avoid any spread of the revolt to Cyprus the Turks took immediate and brutal action. Assembling the island's leading churchmen, including the Archbishop, the Grand Vizier had them summarily executed. The effect of silencing the Greek-Cypriot leadership was achieved: but so was the total alienation of the population from Turkish rule.

After Greece had won her independence, the cracks in the Ottoman Empire began to widen. With the opening of the Suez Canal in 1869 new powers began to flex their muscles in the Mediterranean. The most active of these was the British, who now had a sea-route to India via the Canal. After three dormant centuries Cyprus was suddenly on the map again, and the British began the skilful chess-game that was to bring the island into the Empire as an important strategic base in the Eastern Mediterranean.

In 1877 the war between Russia and Turkey provided the opening move. In return for a defence agreement by which Britain would come to Turkey's aid if Russia made further incursions on Turkish territory, Turkey was to cede Cyprus to Britain. By this agreement – the Anglo-Turkish Convention of 1878 – the British were to remain in occupation of the island as long as the Russian threat continued.

Stavrovouni Monastery

British Period (1878–1960) At a time when one empire – the Ottoman – was reaching its nadir while the other – the British – was reaching its zenith, it was inevitable that the arrangement between the two countries should be indefinitely prolonged, with Cyprus, still nominally a Turkish province, becoming more closely tied to Britain. In 1914, when Turkey joined forces with Germany and Austria-Hungary at the outbreak of World War I, the island was annexed by Britain, who had declared war on Turkey. In the following year they offered the island to Greece as an inducement to that country to enter the war on the side of the allies. Greece, at that time ruled by the pro-German King Constantine and wishing to stay neutral, refused.

The desire of the Greek-Cypriots for a closer link with the mother country remained, however, undiminished. They looked on Greece as the centre of the Hellenic world to which they had belonged for a large part of their history and to which they owed their language, religion and way of life. After Cyprus was made a British Crown Colony in 1925, demands for *Enosis* (Union with Greece) became more strident. In 1931 the first serious riots occurred, resulting in the deportation of a number of Greek-Cypriot leaders, including churchmen. It was the first serious confrontation in an uncertain relationship that was to last for another 30 years.

The Greek-Cypriot resentment of the British was more political than personal. Despite their status as colonial subjects the people of Cyprus enjoyed a rapid material advancement under the British, due to a development of trade and expenditure on public works, farming and communications. During the Second World War Greek-Cypriots fought with the British in Europe and North Africa: since the war more Greek-Cypriots have emigrated to Britain than to any other foreign country. But despite their close association with Britain the Greek-Cypriots remained set on the goal of self-determination for the island.

Opposed to their aims was the Turkish-Cypriot minority, who represent 18% of the population. After the island had been part of Turkey for 300 years, the Turkish-Cypriots were loth to see it handed over to Greece, and were anxious that British rule should be maintained. The British, for their part, were determined to hold on to the island, seeing it as an essential part of their Middle-East defence system.

Leading the *Enosis* campaign, and fulfilling his traditional role of political, as well as religious leadership of his people,

was the Ethnarch of Cyprus, Archbishop Makarios III. Makarios, elected in 1950, conducted the campaign with great vigour, strongly supported by Greece.

In 1954, three events propelled Cyprus towards the inevitable conflict. After the British withdrawal from Egypt their Middle-East HQ was transferred to Cyprus. The Minister of State for the Colonies said in reference to the island: 'There are certain territories in the Commonwealth which . . . can never expect to be fully independent,' And the Greeks, demanding self-determination for Cyprus at the UN, were turned down.

In April, 1955, a series of bomb attacks across the island put an end to the dialogue. It was the beginning of the campaign of violence mounted by the guerilla group EOKA (*Ethniki Organosis Kyprion Agoniston* – The National Organisation of Cypriot Fighters). This group had been organised by an ex-officer of the Greek Army, Colonel George Grivas, in a bid to win *Enosis* for Cyprus. Grivas, who had been born in Cyprus, took the name of a legendary Cypriot hero, Dighenis, and led an armed struggle from secret headquarters in the Troodos. His hit-and-run tactics – bomb attacks, shootings of troops and civilians – provoked a strong reaction from public opinion in Britain, and a series of exhaustive military operations which had limited success, conducted against an elusive foe in a difficult mountain terrain. The imbalance of forces made it a classical example of guerilla warfare: throughout the emergency it is estimated that fewer than 300 EOKA men were holding down security forces numbering 20,000 troops and 4,500 police.

Through their newly-appointed Governor, Field Marshal Sir John Harding, the British pursued a tough line, and in 1956 deported Archbishop Makarios, who had given his blessing to the EOKA campaign and maintained unflinching support for *Enosis* from the pulpit. In 1957, however, under pressure from the United Nations, Britain changed her policy. Makarios was released, though not allowed to return to Cyprus, and Harding was replaced by a civilian Governor, Sir Hugh Foot, whose methods were more conciliatory.

But the expectations of 1957 were dashed by events in 1958. The Turkish-Cypriots, alarmed at the prospect of a British climb-down, commenced a movement for partition and formed their own resistance groups. Clashes between the Turkish and Greek-Cypriot communities, and increased attacks on the British – with civilians as a prime target – made the death toll for 1958 the highest of the emergency and brought matters to a head. Early in 1959 representatives of the British, Greek and Turkish governments met to prepare an agreement for the establishment of an independent Cypriot state within the British Commonwealth, jointly governed by its two communities on a proportional basis. The agreement, which allowed for the retention of two Sovereign Base Areas on the island for the British, was later signed in London by the three powers: Britain, Greece and Turkey, and the two Cypriot leaders: Archbishop Makarios for the Greek-Cypriots, Dr Kutchuk for the Turkish-Cypriots.

The signing of the agreement spelt the end of *Enosis* for the Greeks and partition for the Turks. For the first time in its recorded history, Cyprus had independent rule.

The Cyprus Republic (1960–)   The Republic of Cyprus came into being on August 16th, 1960, with Archbishop Makarios elected as its first President and Dr Kutchuk Vice-President. Under the terms of the Constitution, based on the Zurich and London agreements, the Government and Civil Service of the island were divided 70%–30% between the Greek and Turkish-Cypriots respectively. The same ratio applied to the composition of the police and gendarmerie, and for the army the breakdown was 60% Greek, 40% Turkish. In relation to their population (18%) the Turkish-Cypriots received a favourable share of representation in the island's affairs: a fact that can only be attributed to the proximity and strategic importance of Turkey. The composition of the army was even more controversial, with Greek-Cypriots being asked to serve alongside Turkish-Cypriots who during the Emergency had been auxiliaries in the British Security Forces.

In its anxiety to protect the interests of the Turkish-Cypriot minority, the Constitution favoured it in other ways. The Turkish-Cypriot Vice-President shared the President's right of veto over policies affecting foreign affairs, defence or internal security. Under the Constitution, a Bill could only be passed by a majority of votes from both sides of the House of Representatives. In the ratio of 35 Greeks to 15 Turks, this meant that eight Turks could defeat any bill. A further concession to the Turkish-Cypriots was the establishment of separate municipal services for each community in the five major towns: this rapidly proved unworkable.

In 1963 Archbishop Makarios proposed 13 amendments to the Constitution, including the abolition of his and Dr Kutchuk's right of veto, the abolition of separate majority voting in the House, the abolition of separate municipalities and the adjustment of ratios in public services and the armed forces. The Turkish Government, to which these proposals were submitted, immediately rejected them. A deterioration in the relations between Greece and Turkey and between the two communities in Cyprus followed, and in December 1963 the first fighting broke out between Greek and Turkish-Cypriots in Nicosia. The Turks withdrew from the Government, the Civil Service, police and army and set up a separate administration in their own enclaves.

After renewed fighting the following year a UN peace-keeping force was sent to Cyprus (March 1974) but was unable to prevent the series of incidents that culminated in the tragic events of 1974.

On July 15 of that year a coup engineered by the junta in Greece and carried out by the Greek-officered National Guard overthrew the government of President Makarios. The president was forced to flee the island and a puppet regime was imposed under a former EOKA man, Nicos Samson. Samson had been active against the Turks after independence, and the presence of a pro-Enosis regime in the island, with its threat to the future safety of the Turkish-Cypriots, was highly provocative to the Turks.

Under the Treaty of Guarantee signed by Britain, Greece and Turkey in 1960, empowering them to act jointly or unilaterally to combat any threat to the Constitution, Turkey exercised her right to take military action.

On July 21 1974 the Turkish army invaded Cyprus and occupied 40% of its territory, north of a line from Morphou Bay running through the centre of Nicosia and down to Famagusta, sealing off the Greek area of Varosha.

A transfer of populations followed, with Greek-Cypriots in the north fleeing to the south and Turkish-Cypriots in the south going to the north. Although the puppet regime collapsed and the legitimate government was restored, the Turks did not withdraw but revealed the true object of their invasion, the enclosure of their own people in a separate part of the island.

The Republic of Cyprus, which officially represents the whole of the island, now controls only 60%. Its President is Mr Spyros Kyprianou, who succeeded Makarios after his death (1977). The Turkish 'Federated State' in the north, financed largely by Turkey, has no international recognition. Its leader is Mr Rauf Denktash.

The UN presence is maintained as a buffer between the two communities.

Practical information

TRAVEL TO CYPRUS

By air

The two airlines offering direct flights to Cyprus from the UK are **Cyprus Airways** and **British Airways**. In the high season (1 Apr–31 Oct) there is a minimum of two daily flights from London (Heathrow) to Larnaca (flight time 4hrs). In the low season (1 Nov–31 Mar) there is a minimum of one daily flight. From Manchester there are twice weekly flights in the summer, once weekly in winter.

The cheapest flights to the island are those offered by tourist excursion return fares. These are valid for a minimum stay of 7 days and a maximum stay of 42 days.

Details of fares and timetables from:

Cyprus Airways Euston Centre, 29/31 Hampstead Rd, London NW1

Olympic Airways offer a through service of four flights a week in the summer (15 Jun–31 Oct) London–Athens–Larnaca. An overnight stay in Athens is necessary on other flights.

By sea

There are no cruises to Cyprus from the UK, but services are operated throughout the high season (Apr–Oct) by the following steamship companies (routes in brackets):

CTC Lines (Black Sea Shipping Co)
1 Regent St, London SW1
(Odessa–Istanbul–Piraeus–Larnaca–Lattakia–Alexandria)

Louis Tourist Agency 429 Green Lanes, London N4
(Piraeus–Rhodes–Limassol–Alexandria)

Sol Shipping Cyprus Travel (London) 36 Hampstead Rd, London NW1
(Venice–Piraeus–Rhodes–Limassol–Haifa)

Zenon Travel & Tours 15 Kentish Town Rd, London NW1
(Piraeus–Heraklion–Limassol–Haifa)

The land-sea journey, of course, requires more travelling time. The Brindisi–Larnaca voyage, for example, takes 3 days and a further 40 hours would have to be allowed for the rail trip from London to Brindisi.

ACCESS TO NORTHERN CYPRUS

The northern part of the island, which includes the districts of Kyrenia and Famagusta, is under Turkish Military occupation and no longer a legitimate tourist area. The Government of the Republic of Cyprus, which is internationally recognised as the lawful government of the island, has declared the ports of Famagusta, Kyrenia and Karavostassi, as well as Ercan airport as prohibited points of entry into the Republic. Any person travelling through these ports and airports is therefore *persona non grata* in the Republic of Cyprus.

Tourists wishing to visit the north of the island from the south may do so at their own discretion, but no responsibility can be accepted by the Government of Cyprus or any travel organisation for those individuals who cross to the north.

The formalities of entering the Turkish-occupied territory from the south involve presentation of a passport, application for a travel permit (limit two days) and re-insurance of any vehicle hired in the south.

TRAVEL IN CYPRUS

Cyprus has no railways but an excellent road system. Problems were, however, caused by the division of the island and some of the direct routes (Nicosia–Larnaca, Nicosia–Troodos) had to be diverted. Since 1974 considerable pressure has been put on the road between Nicosia and the developing port and resort of Limassol in the south, and a new road is nearing completion. For the motorist wishing to get into the mountains there are fast routes to the central Troodos via Peristerona (from Nicosia) or via Polemidhia (from Limassol).

Bus services are available between towns and villages but have these limitations: a) the inter-town buses do not run at night and b) the village buses run only early in the morning to take the villagers to market, returning at midday. Timetables are available at the offices of the bus companies (shown as 'B' on the maps of the main towns in this guide).

The most satisfactory way of seeing the island is undoubtedly by **car**, whether it is the traveller's own car, a hired, self-drive car or a shared taxi. An alternative is to take one of the sightseeing tours offered by the agencies listed.

Road signs in Cyprus are bilingual, with English equivalents to the Greek names. Two excellent road maps are available, though only from the main bookshops (one of the best bookshops in Nicosia for guides and maps is the Moufflon in Sophoulis St, Nicosia). The first is the compact $\frac{1}{4}$-inch to the mile *Survey of Cyprus Administration Map*, based on the Ordnance Survey, and the second, on a slightly smaller scale, the Clyde Surveys *Leisure Map of Cyprus*, which shows tourist facilities in the island and includes town plans of Nicosia, Limassol, Larnaca and Paphos.

Roads

The categories of road in the island are a) motorway b) single lane c) unmade. Before he becomes too intrigued by the spidery lines on the map which lead to the remoter corners of the island, the car-borne explorer should be warned about this third category, usually described on maps as 'other roads'. The standard of these roads, which are unsurfaced, varies enormously. The forest road which runs from Kykko to Stavros tis Psokas, although slow (15–20mph) is well maintained and only hazardous after heavy rain, when fallen rocks may cause an obstruction. The views of the northern flank of the Troodos are superb on this route, which can be continued southwards to Paphos.

The unmade roads to some of the remoter churches and monasteries are, however, to be tackled with caution. To prevent them washing away in the wet weather the surfaces are laid with stones and rubble, which can work loose and cause a bumpy ride. Before attempting them drivers should check their spare wheel and jacking equipment.

New roads have been constructed from Platres to Troodos (replacing the old 'Seven Sisters' hairpin bends) and from Nicosia to Limassol. Outside towns and villages (30mph) the speed limit is 50mph.

A final word of encouragement to British motorists – in Cyprus they drive on the left!

Petrol

Petrol is roughly the same price in Cyprus as in the UK. An important point to remember is that petrol stations in the island are closed from 4pm on Saturday until Monday morning.

Driving formalities

The only requirement for visitors who wish to drive in Cyprus is a valid driving licence. Motorists bringing their own vehicle to the island will require in addition a Green International Insurance Card (from their insurance company) and a Certificate of Foreign Insurance. The latter may be obtained free of charge, from the Regis-

trar of Motor Vehicles, 24 Byron Avenue, Nicosia, by either personal or postal application (in either case, a Green Card must be submitted). The Carnet and Temporary Export Certificate are no longer required for vehicles entering Cyprus, but visitors' cars may not be kept in the island for more than six months.

Self-drive cars

Most car-hire firms in Cyprus offer the following as part of their service:

1. Full insurance (this can exclude the first £250 of any damage sustained).
2. Delivery to port, airport or hotel to meet the visitor on arrival.
3. If a car-hire company has several offices in different parts of the island the car does not have to be returned to the office from which it was issued, but may be left at any of these branch offices.
4. Unlimited mileage, i.e. no additional charge per mile driven.
5. Oil and maintenance.

The cost of car hire in Cyprus varies from £10-£13 per day depending on the make of car, the period of hire and the season. If collision damage waiver is required to avoid damage costs (see 1, above) there is an additional charge of £3 per day. All the major towns have car-hire firms.

Sightseeing tours

Firms offering daily excursions by coach to places of interest in Cyprus can be located in all the major towns. The main agencies are:

Aeolos Tours Nicosia, Limassol, Larnaca, Paphos, Ayia Napa
Holiday Tours Nicosia, Limassol, Larnaca, Paphos
Hull, Blyth, Araouzos Ltd Nicosia, Limassol, Larnaca
Louis Tourist Agency Ltd Nicosia, Limassol, Larnaca, Paphos, Paralimni

Taxis

Taxis are metered with an initial charge of 25 cents (slightly more at night). The rates are 15 cents per mile for round trips and 19 cents per mile for single trips. For a 'service taxi' for 4-7 persons the rates are reduced. These are shared taxis or mini-buses in which a single seat may be reserved in advance through your hotel. The taxi will come to the hotel, take you to your destination and then, if a round trip is required, the same company will pick you up at an agreed place and time and return you to your hotel. This service is usually available every ½ hour and there is no extra charge for coming to the hotel.

Inclusive holidays

A package tour including flight, accommodation and food is the quickest and cheapest way of holidaying in Cyprus. The airlines serving the island from the UK – Cyprus Airways and British Airways – are currently offering package holidays in association with tour operators. Lists of UK tour operators offering package holidays to Cyprus are available from the Cyprus Tourism Organisation, 211/3 Regent St, London W1. The varied choice includes the two-centre holiday (i.e. staying at more than one resort) and those including a self-drive car. Self-catering accommodation is also available. The main tour operators specialising in Cyprus are:

Amathus Holidays 51 Tottenham Court Rd, London W1

Cyplon Travel 563 Green Lanes, London N8

Cyprair 21 Hampstead Rd, London NW1

Cypriana Holidays 148 Kentish Town Rd, London NW1

Cyprustours 21 Sussex St, London SW1

Cyprus Travel Club Boadicea House, 132 Greyhound Rd, London W6

Delta Travel University Precinct, Oxford Rd, Manchester

Excel Holidays 285-7 Grays Inn Rd, London WC1

Exchange Travel Holidays Exchange House, Parker Rd, Hastings, Sussex

Kypros Travel 190/190A Camden High St, London NW1

Lanes Travel Service 251 Brompton Rd, London SW3

Libra Travel 15/16 Newman St, London W1

Nicholas Bros (Travel) 88 Camden High St, London NW1

Olympic Holidays 17 Old Court Place, High St, Kensington, London W8

Seagull Holidays 46 Maddox St, London W1

Sovereign Holidays PO Box 410, West London Air Terminal, Cromwell Rd, London SW7

Sunvil Travel Sunvil House, 88 Sheen Rd, Richmond, Surrey

Thomas Cook 45 Berkeley St, London W1

Thomson Holidays Greater London House, Hampstead Rd, London NW1

ACCOMMODATION

Hotels

In recent years there have been rapid advances in hotel development in Cyprus. All hotels are graded to comply with international standards and details of classification and prices are included in a complete list of hotels, the *Cyprus Hotels Guide*, published annually by the Cyprus Tourism Organisation.

A list of hotels appears on p. 29.

Hill resorts

The hill resorts of Cyprus provide an agreeable contrast to the coastal resorts – particularly during the hot months from July to September (high season) when the higher altitudes offer a fresher, cooler look at the island to the holidaymaker in search of a change of climate and scenery.

For these individuals the ideal 2-week summer holiday would be one that combined a week in a coastal resort with a week in the mountains (the village of Platres at 4000' above sea level in the Troodos range offers the widest choice of hotels). A number of tour operators are now offering these combined two-centre holidays (summer only).

The hill resort of Troodos (5,500'), the highest in the island, is particularly popular in the winter months for skiing (Jan–March). At this time of year one can enjoy the unique experience of snow skiing on Troodos at an altitude of around 6000' and water-skiing in the Mediterranean (1½ hours' distance by car) on the same day.

The following hill resorts all offer hotel accommodation:

Troodos
Platres
Prodhromos
Pedhoulas
Kalopanayiotis
Kakopetria
Perapedhi
Agros

Accommodation is also available at **Stavros tis Psokas** Forest Station (western Troodos) for up to three nights, although this is not a resort.

Villas and apartments

Rather than stay in hotels many holidaymakers prefer to rent a villa or apartment. This gives them a greater degree of freedom and privacy, and need not involve any undesired work, such as cleaning or catering. The amount of work that one wishes to undertake, in fact, is a matter of choice. Many of the apartments offered by tour operators (like those of Lordos) are run on the lines of a hotel, with a daily maid service. As far as catering is concerned, those who wish to use the facilities of their holiday home for cooking will find plenty of good shops in the main centres, with a choice of local and imported foods. Eating out, however, is no problem, with many reasonable restaurants available in towns and villages.

These villas and apartments can – like the hotels – be booked privately, but it is worth noting that they are also available as part of an inclusive holiday (with return air flight, and self-drive car if required) in most travel brochures. Private bookings may be made through estate agents in Cyprus, whose tariffs are obtainable at travel agents.

Camping

Three organised camp sites are currently operating in Cyprus in the following areas:

Ayia Napa
Troodos resort
Pyla (near sea 3 miles east of Larnaca)
Polis (in eucalyptus forest near sea)

These sites all offer toilets, showers etc. Anyone wishing to camp elsewhere in the island must obtain permission from the local District Officer, who may be contacted through the nearest police station. The District Officers have given permission to some restaurant owners at coastal resorts to operate a camp site with basic facilities around their premises.

Youth hostels

Information on current youth hostel facilities available in Cyprus may be obtained from the Cyprus Youth Hostels Association, PO Box 1328, Nicosia, Cyprus. There are Youth Hostels at Nicosia, Limassol, Paphos, Troodos and Stavros tis Psokas Forest Station. Visitors wishing to stay at these hostels should be in possession of an International Youth Hostel card.

Monasteries

Overnight accommodation is offered to visitors at most of the monasteries. There is no catering, but simple food is usually obtainable from local cafés. Accommodation at monasteries is free of charge, but an offering should be made by visitors.

FOOD AND DRINK

The pleasure of eating out in Cyprus is best summed up by the familiar sight of the owner of a roadside café going out to the yard at the back to pick fresh lemons for his customer's *kebab*.

This is the essence of Cypriot food, for in addition to his lemon tree the café owner will have at his disposal a freshly killed lamb from the village butcher, fresh vegetables for the salad, oven-baked *pita* (bread envelopes) a local yoghourt, and a bottle of cold Cypriot *rosé*. The *kebab*, and everything that goes with it, comes from Cyprus' own back yard, a special feature of the island's gastronomy that makes it so attractive for visitors from Northern Europe.

On a grander scale is Cyprus' most popular speciality, the *meze*. This began as a

snack served with drinks: now the drinks are served with the *meze*, a varied and tantalising feast of several courses. The *meze* can be enjoyed anywhere in Cyprus, in village taverns or city restaurants. The variety of courses and the sophistication of the service depends of course of the choice of restaurant.

A good *meze* should not cost more than £3–4 (add £1 for a bottle of local wine). The ingredients are, quite simply, the fruits of the Cypriot soil, which should stimulate the most jaded northern palate.

A *meze* can have one to four courses, which each offer a variety of dishes. The secret of the *meze*, which takes a little practice to uncover (can one imagine a more pleasant pursuit?) is to discover which particular combinations offer the most complementary flavours. The rule, if there must be one, is not to plough your way through every single dish — or you'll never get past the first course!

A typical Cypriot *meze* would contain a selection of the following dishes:

First course (*hors d'oeuvres*)
Halloumi Cheese peculiar to Cyprus, of slight rubbery texture
Feta Sourish white cheese made from sheep's milk
Talattouri Cucumber and yoghourt
Tahina Sesame relish
Houmos Chick peas crushed with olive oil, garlic and parsley
Taramosalata Relish of ground cod's roe, highly spiced
Dolmas Stuffed vine leaves
Olives, sliced and pickled vegetables
Sliced meats, usually turkey, salami or ham

Second course (cooked meats etc.)
Tavas Meat, onion and herbs, cooked and served in earthenware bowls
Moussaka Oven-baked savoury pie of minced meat with herbs, aubergines and other vegetables
Stifado Beef or veal stewed with onions
Patcha Lamb stewed with lemon and garlic
Pork afelia Marinated pork, braised or fried
Zalatina Pork brawn
Keftedes Highly-spiced meat balls

Third course (*kebab*, or in Greek *souvlaki*)
Either chicken or meat *kebab* is served, (sometimes both). The meat is charcoal-grilled, either lamb or pork often with liver and *sheftalia*, a sausage of minced meat and onion.

Fourth course (dessert)
This is usually fruit, which in Cyprus is plentiful and varied, according to the

season. Alternatively one may find a choice of Cypriot sweetmeats, many of Greek or Turkish origin:

Soujoukko A popular sweetmeat made by dipping strings of nuts in warm grape juice, which dries into long globular sticks

Lokmades Hot doughnuts served in syrup

Kataif Shredded sweetmeat, with almonds and syrup

Baclava Sweet pastry

Halva Cake made with semolina and almonds

Loukoumia Turkish delight

This list of dishes gives an idea of the range of Cypriot food. Most of those in the second and third courses can be enjoyed on their own, as a separate meal. Fish is scarce in Cyprus and is most common in restaurants in the south of the island, notably in Paphos and Limassol. Here one may sample a fish *meze* which might consist of:

Barbounia Red mullet

Kalamares Baby squid

Marides Whitebait

Oktapodi Octopus (boiled)

Drink

Cyprus is noted for the range of its wines, which have something to offer every palate. The most famous and the most historic is the sweet dessert wine **Commandaria**. Originally produced by the Crusader knights, this has been a popular drink in Cyprus since the 13th c. Other wines produced in the island include the light dry **Keo hock**, which goes well with a *meze*, the vintage white table wine **Aphrodite**, the sweet white **St Panteleimon**, the gentle rosé wines (**Coeur de Lion**, Rosella), the dry red **Domaine d'Ahera** and the popular **Othello**, also produced by Keo, which is similar to burgundy. On the subject of wine it is worth noting that there are no small bottles available in restaurants. This is, perhaps, a compliment from the Cypriots to their wine: but it must be pointed out that however much he enjoys it, there is no obligation for the customer to finish the whole bottle. He will be charged only for what he drinks.

The Cypriots' favourite aperitif is *ouzo*, the clear aniseed drink that turns white when mixed with water. This is a popular drink, under different names, throughout the Middle East. If there were a national drink, it would be Cypriot brandy, which is very good and very cheap. A favourite application of it is in brandy sour, where the brandy is mixed with lemon squash, sugar, soda water and Angostura bitters. A refreshing light beer is produced by Keo of Limassol, which is also one of the main wine factories.

Turkish coffee is most commonly served, the alternative being the ubiquitous Nescafé. A glass of water always accompanies the coffee, which is served *glykos* 'sweet', *metrios* 'medium' or *sketos* 'unsweetened'.

Restaurants

The gastronomic notes to the island of Cyprus all give the same advice. If you want to stick to the familiar, i.e. international food, stay in your hotel. If you want to sample the variety of Cypriot food described above you must do a little exploring.

Because the food in Cyprus is so reasonable, selection is based less on prices than on atmosphere and taste. In Nicosia, for example, it is possible to adapt the style of the evening to your mood — and appetite. A meal in Lemonias' (Charlie's Bar) is full of noise, cheerful waiters, a bewildering succession of succulent dishes. The Greek Tavern offers music, Greek and local dishes, sophistication. The open-air kebab-stalls in the moat near Liberty Square offer candlelight, plastic tablecloths, a good earthy wine and the best *souvlaki* in town. Those who enjoy a dinner-dance in elegant surroundings will like the Cosmopolitan, one of Nicosia's most popular night spots. Wherever you go you'll be sure not only of a delicious meal but an evening to remember.

Some popular restaurants

Nicosia

Corner Demetris Severis Ave

Cosmopolitan (night club) Grivas Dighenis Ave

Ekali Ayios Spyridon St

Garden Café (opp. Museum) for snacks

Greek Tavern Grivas Dighenis Ave

Lemonias (Charlie's Bar) Ipatias Lycavitos St

Makedonitissa 3m. west of Nicosia off airport road

Theo's Larnaca St

Larnaca

Ambiance G. Afxentiou Ave

Dolphin Athens Ave

Kimon Athens Ave

Helioupolis Lord Byron St

Theo's Athens Ave

Limassol

Avenida Limassol–Nicosia road

Ladas (fish restaurant) Sadi St (near old harbour)

Trans Taverna 28 October St

Fish restaurants at the Pendadromos

Pissouri village
(between Limassol and Paphos)
Bunch of Grapes Inn

Ayia Napa
Fish restaurants on the beach

Paphos
Kato Paphos harbour has three good fish restaurants:
Pelican Inn, Theo's, King's
Also in Kato Paphos:
Castle Tavern, Chimney, Myra
In Ktima:
Nikandros Makarios III Ave

CLIMATE

For most of the year the island enjoys constant sunshine. The hottest months (Jul–Sept) are best spent on the coast, where the sea breezes abate the heat and one can make the most of the wonderful bathing. Inland, the temperature in the plain around Nicosia at the height of summer can touch 100°F/38°C. By contrast, the temperature in the mountains is usually 20°F/–6.7°C lower and the hill resorts are recommended as an alternative to the coast at this time of year.

The first rain after the summer drought usually falls in October, and the heaviest rainfall is between December and February. Temperatures in these winter months average 50°F/10°C. The best time to visit Cyprus is either spring or autumn.

SPORT AND ENTERTAINMENT

The greatest recreation for visitors to Cyprus, summer and winter, is provided by its superb and varied coastline, which with the exception of the less accessible western shore offers an endless choice of attractive beaches and the accompanying pleasure of a warm, gentle sea (water temperature ranging from 60°F/15.5°C in January to 80°F/26.7°C in July) ideal for swimming and water sports. Some of the best beaches are the most isolated, but all the sea resorts are within easy reach of beaches that are among the best in the Mediterranean. Facilities for water sports – sailing, water skiing, wind surfing and underwater swimming – are available at most resorts.

Popular beaches

Larnaca has one of the best beach areas in Cyprus, stretching around the bay to the east of the town. The southern end is dominated by the oil refinery and most of the hotel development is further along towards Dhekelia. This is the location of the Larnaca Tourist Beach (6m. from Larnaca) organised by the Tourism Organisation with a restaurant, bar and swimming facilities. The town has a small beach next to the marina.

Limassol also has a Tourist Beach, 3m. east of the town (Dassoudi). To the west the nearest popular beach is 'Ladies Mile', reached by taking the south-west exit of the town signposted 'Zakaki' and then turning left towards the sea. Further west, beyond Curium, the coastline is more rocky and there is a succession of bays with pebbled beaches, enclosed by towering white cliffs. The most accessible of these are in the British Sovereign Base Area. Midway between Limassol and Paphos is the famous Bay of Aphrodite with its landmark of rock broken into the sea (Petra tou Romiou). This could not be a more perfect spot in which to emulate the Goddess of Love 'on the waves of the sea . . . amid the soft foam.'

Paphos has good swimming both to the east and west of the old city (Nea Paphos). The shoreline is rocky and undeveloped and should appeal to those seeking a secluded bathe. 7 m north of

Soujoukko

Paphos, on the west coast, is the beautiful Coral Bay, its beach tinged with fragmented pink coral. Yeroskipos, 2m. east of Paphos, has a new Tourist Beach.

Pissouri Beach, 25m. west of Limassol, lies in an attractive sandy bay in the lee of Cape Aspro. It is best reached from the main road (2m.).

Ayia Napa has two excellent sandy beaches. The one to the east of the village is the location of the Grecian Bay Hotel, and that to the west, with attractive sand dunes, the Nissi Beach Hotel and Bungalows.

Paralimni on the east coast, a newly-developing area, has a more rocky coastline, but with sandy coves.

Winter sports

Between January and March the snow-covered Troodos Mountains offer perfect conditions for skiing and other winter sports. By joining the Cyprus Ski Club in Nicosia as a temporary member the winter holidaymaker can obtain all the required facilities: instructor, ski-hire, etc.

Entertainment

There is no shortage of entertainment in the principal resorts. Night clubs or cabarets are not exclusively expensive and the universal discotheque is now a feature of the island's night life. There are plenty of cinemas, both indoor and outdoor (summer only) showing international films. But for a rounded evening's entertainment the visitor need look no further than a good local restaurant which may offer, in addition to its interesting food and friendly atmosphere, a helping of bouzouki and folk-dancing.

FOLK ART

Most folk art in Cyprus represents a continuing tradition of craftsmanship, going back many centuries. but in the age of mass production it is inevitable that some of these crafts have died out. One of the lost crafts is **wood carving**, examples of which can now only be seen in a few houses and in folk art museums. Designs were usually engraved on the large walnut chests in which the family linen was kept (often for the dowry), or on shelves, chairs or beds. The designs – usually geometrical or stylised flowers, animals etc., were often painted in red, blue and green.

Pottery is the oldest Cypriot craft, first introduced in the Stone Age. Modern potters copy the styles of early periods, particularly the elaborate designs of the Early Bronze Age, but this is usually for souvenirs. The most common pottery made in Cyprus today is the purely functional type, made in such centres as Kornos and Phini. These are the large storage jars, many of them still thrown on foot-operated wheels, which are used for storing oil and wine. The more decorative, non-traditional pottery suitable for gifts can be bought in many parts of the island. A good pottery is *Savvas*, whose workshop is just outside Paphos on the Limassol road (also in Kato Paphos).

The traditional art most readily associated with the island is **embroidery**, which has been a Cypriot handicraft for at least five centuries. The finest embroidery is done by the women of the villages of Pano and Kato Lefkara and is known as *lefkaritika*. This is often mistakenly referred to as 'lace', when in fact it is a very fine needlework, usually done on Irish linen, with patterns derived from the Venetian needlework of the 16th c. This beautiful embroidery may be bought anywhere in Cyprus, but if time allows, visitors are recommended to go to Lefkara where they will get the biggest choice and the most reasonable prices from the lace merchants' shops. During the summer

Women embroidering, Pano Lefkara

26

months they will also have the pleasure of seeing the women of Lefkara at work on their embroidery in the streets of the two villages.

Other Cypriot crafts are **weaving**, **basketwork** and **silver** and **copper work**.

POPULAR FESTIVALS

January 6
Feast of the Submersion of the Holy Cross
This takes place in all the coastal towns in commemoration of the Epiphany of the Holy Spirit.

February/March
Limassol Carnival (50 days before Easter)
Larnaca Procession of the Icon of St Lazarus (30 Mar)

April/May
Easter celebrations including the procession of the Epitaphios on Good Friday, an impressive part of the Greek Orthodox festival.
Flower festivals throughout the island (early May)
Cataclysmos This festival, celebrated on the seashore in the coastal towns, is a survival of an early pagan ritual associated with the birth of Aphrodite.

June/July
Nicosia Festival (mid-Jun)
Paphos St Paul's Feast (end of Jun)
Limassol International Art Festival (early Jul)
Curium Performances of Shakespeare and ancient Greek drama throughout the summer at the Roman theatre

August
Dormition of the Holy Virgin At Kykko and Troodhitissa monasteries (mid-Aug)

September
Limassol Wine Festival (mid-Sep)

LANGUAGE

Although the native tongue of the Greek-Cypriots is Greek there is an inheritance of English from the British occupation and this is taught in schools.

Most Cypriots that the visitor is likely to meet – hotel and shopkeepers, street-traders, etc., are likely to know some English, but knowledge of the Greek words for numbers is recommended for those intending to shop in village markets. In addition, it should be remembered that the use of the language of a country is always an act of courtesy. When a villager calls 'Kalimera' ('Good Morning') a reply in like manner will please your Cypriot host.

WEIGHT

For shopping it is useful to remember that the basic unit of weight in Cyprus is the dram. 100 drams = 11.2 oz. and 400 drams or 1 oke = 2.83 lbs.

CURRENCY AND BANKS

The Cyprus pound is divided into 100 cents, with denominations as follows:

Notes: £10, £5, £1, 50 cents
Coins: 100, 50, 25, 5 cents

Foreign money and travellers' cheques can be changed at exchange bureaux, banks and at the main hotels. Branches of the island's largest bank, the Bank of Cyprus, are in all the major towns. Banking hours are usually 09.00–12.00 (except Sundays and holidays). Some banks in the main towns and resorts offer a special afternoon service for tourists, from 14.00–17.00.

GUIDE AND REFERENCE BOOKS

An excellent series of guides to the excavations, castles and other ancient monuments of Cyprus is published by the Cyprus Department of Antiquities. The guides contain maps and detailed descriptions of the sites and are available at the office of the custodian.

For specialised reading on Cyprus the following books are recommended:

Recent politics
Cyprus Revolt: An Account of the Struggle for Union with Greece by Nancy Crawshaw (Allen & Unwin, 1978)

History
Cyprus in History: A Survey of 5000 years by Doros Alastos (Zeno, 1976)
Cyprus by H. D. Purcell (Benn, 1969)

Archaeology
Cyprus: Archaeologia Mundi Series by V. Karageorghis (Nagel, 1968)

Byzantine churches
The Painted Churches of Cyprus by A. & J. Stylianou (Nicosia, 1964)

General interest
Cyprus: A Portrait and an Appreciation by Sir Harry Luke (Harrap, 1957)
Bitter Lemons by Lawrence Durrell (Faber & Faber, 1957)
Journey into Cyprus by Colin Thubron (Heinemann, 1975)

Two good bookshops in London specialising in Cyprus books are: Zeno of Denmark St, WC1 and Hellenic Book Services, 122 Charing Cross Rd, WC2

TOURIST INFORMATION

All information on Cyprus is available from the **Cyprus Tourism Organisation, 211/213 Regent St, London W1.**

Tourist Information Offices in Cyprus:
Larnaca 24-hr service at airport also in town at Democratias Square
Nicosia 5 Princess de Tyras St
Limassol 15 Spyros Araouzos St
Paphos 3 Gladstone St

MUSEUMS AND MONUMENTS

Ancient monuments and museums are in the custody of the Cyprus Department of Antiquities, whose headquarters is at the Cyprus Museum, Nicosia. Entrance is usually 20 cents. Visiting hours for museums and monuments (closed on public holidays) are:

MUSEUMS

Summer
(mid May–end Aug)

Winter
(early Sep–mid May)

Nicosia: Cyprus Museum
Limassol: District Museum
Paphos: District Museum

Daily: 08.00-13.30	Daily: 07.30-14.00
16.00-18.00	15.00-17.00
Sun: 10.00-13.00	Sat: 07.30-13.00
	15.00-17.00
	Sun: 10.00-13.00

Larnaca: District Museum
Episkopi: Kourion Museum
Yeroskipos: Folk Art Museum

Mon-Sat: 07.30-13.30	Mon-Fri: 07.30-14.00
	Sat: 07.30-13.00

Nicosia: Byzantine Museum

Mon-Fri: 09.30-17.30	Mon-Fri: 09.00-17.00
Sat: 09.00-13.00	Sat: 09.00-13.00
Sun: 10.00-13.00	Sun: 10.00-13.00

Nicosia: Folk Art Museum

Mon-Fri: 08.00-13.30	Mon-Fri: 08.00-13.00
15.00-17.30	14.00-16.30
Sat: 08.00-13.00	Sat: 08.00-13.00

ANCIENT MONUMENTS & SITES

Larnaca: Kition ancient site, Hala Sultan Tekke, Khirokitia ancient site

Limassol: Kolossi Castle, Curium ancient site and Sanctuary of Apollo

Paphos: Royal Tombs and Roman mosaics at Nea Paphos, Palea Paphos ancient site

Daily: 07.30-dusk throughout year

Summer	**Winter**

Limassol Castle

Mon-Sat: 07.30-13.30	Mon-Fri: 07.30-14.00
	Sat: 07.30-13.00

Larnaca Fort

Mon-Sat: 07.30-19.30	Mon-Sat: 07.30-17.00

Paphos Fort

Mon-Sat: 07.30-13.30	Mon-Fri: 07.30-14.00
	Sat: 07.30-13.00

Peyia ancient site
Tamassos ancient site

Tue-Sun: 09.00-12.00	Tue-Sun: 09.00-13.00
16.00-19.00	14.00-16.30

Aphrodite from Soli, Cyprus Museum

HOTELS

Nicosia

5-star
Cyprus Hilton Makarios III Ave

4-star
Churchill 1 Achaeans St
Ledra Grivas Dighenis Ave
Philoxenia Evlenya Ave

3-star
Asty 12 Prince Charles St
Cleopatra 8 Florina St
Europa 16 Alceos St
Excelsior 4 Photios Stavrou Pitta St
Kennedy 70 Regaena St
Lido 6/8 Philokypros St

2-star
Acropole 17 Heroes St
Averof 11 Averof St
Catsellis Hill 11 Kasos St
Crown 13 Philellinon St
Nicosia Palace 6/8 C. Pantelides Ave

1-star
Alexandria 17 Trikoupi St
Carlton 13 Princess de Tyras St
City 209 Ledra St
Elsy 11 Chiou St
Pisa Tower 33 Ayios Nicolaos St, Engomi
Regina Palace 8/12 Regaena St
Sans Rival 7G, Solonos St
Venetian Walls 38 Ouzounian St

Hotels without star/guest houses
Alasia 23 Pigmalion St
Cottage 13 Orpheos St, Ayios Dhometios
Delphi 24 C. Pantelides Ave
Femina 114 Ledra St
Gardenia 23 Regaena St
Kypros 16A Vass. Voulgaroktonos St
Peters 5 Solonos St
Royal 17 Euripides St

Limassol

5-star
Amathus Beach 6m. east of Limassol
Apollonia Beach 4m. east of Limassol
Poseidonia Beach 4m. east of Limassol

4-star
Churchill Limassol 28 October Ave
Curium Palace Byron St
Limonia Bay 7m. east of Limassol
Miramare 2m. east of Limassol

3-star
Adonia Beach 6m. east of Limassol
Alasia 1 Haydari St
Ariadne 333 28 October Ave
Arsinoe 4m. east of Limassol
Asteria Beach Potamos Yermassoyias
Astir 142 Anexartissias St
Avenida Beach 7m. east of Limassol
Crusader Beach 2m. east of Limassol
Kanika Beach 28 October Ave
Kanika Twin Pan. Symeou St
King Richard 5m. east of Limassol

Larnaca

4-star
Golden Bay Larnaca-Dhekelia road
Palm Beach Larnaca-Dhekelia road
Sun Hall Athens Ave

3-star
Beau Rivage Larnaca-Dhekelia road
Flamingo Piale Pasha St
Four Lanterns 19 Athens Ave
Karpasiana Beach Larnaca-Dhekelia road
Lordos Beach Larnaca-Dhekelia road

2-star
Arion 26 Galileo St
Bellapais Pervolia Larnacos
Ioanna Larnaca-Dhekelia road
Mariandy Larnaca-Dhekelia road
Sandbeach Castle Piale Pasha St

1-star
Pavion 11 St Lazarus Sq

Hotels without star/guest houses
La Maison Belge 103 Stadious St
Harry's Inn 75 Athens Ave
The Rainbow Inn 140 Zenonos Kitios St

Paphos

4-star
Paphos Beach Ayios Antonios St

3-star
Aloe St Antonios St
Cynthiana Beach Kissonerga
(5m. north of Paphos)
Dionysos 1 Poseidon St
Kissos Tombs of the Kings Rd
Paphiana Konia
Pavemar 28 October Ave
Pissouri Beach Pissouri Bay
(25m. west of Limassol)

2-star
Aquamarina
Chez Nous 4m. east of Limassol
Pefkos 86 Kavazoglou St
Sunny Beach 28 October Ave
Trans 5m. east of Limassol

1-star
Continental 137 Spyros Araouzos St
Le Village 220 Leontios A St
Limassol Palace 97/99 Spyros Araouzos St
Panorama 36 Pavlos Melas St

Hotels without star/guest houses
Acropole 21 George Malikides St
Arizona 31 Mesolongion St
Astoria 13A George Malikides St
Bunch of Grapes Inn Pissouri
(25m. west of Limassol)
Excelsior 35 Anexartisias St
Habra Epirus St
Hellas 9 Zig Zag St
Icaros 61 Eleftherias St
Kallithea 12 Simos Menardos St
Luxor 101 Ayios Andreas St
Metropole 6 Iphigenia St
Rose 50 Zenon St
Vienna 71 Vass. Macedona St

2-star
Apollo St Paul's Ave
Axiothea 2 Aeolos St
Kings Hotel Tombs of the Kings Rd
Marion Polis
(38m. north of Paphos)
Melina II Off St Paul's Ave
New Olympus 12 Byron St
Theofano Ayios Antonios St

1-star
Agapinor 24 St Paul's Ave
Pyramos 4 Ayios Anastasias St

Hotels without star/guest houses
Kinyras 89 Makarios Ave
Paphos Palace 10 Grivas Dighenis Ave
Pelican Inn 102 St Paul's Ave
Trianon 99 Makarios Ave

Ayia Napa
5-star **Grecian Bay**
4-star **Asterias Beach, Florida**
3-star **Marina, Nissi Beach, Nissi Park**
1-star **Leros**

Paralimni
4-star **Sunrise Beach, Vrissiana Beach**
2-star **Pernera Beach**

HILL RESORTS

Platres
4-star **Forest Park**
2-star **Edelweiss, Pendeli**
1-star **Grand, Lanterns Cottage, Minęrva, Splendid**

Hotels without star/guest houses
Kallithea, Mount Royal, New Helvetia, Pafsilypon, Petit Palais, Semiramis, Spring, Vienna

Troodos
2-star **Jubilee, Troodos**

Prodhromos
1-star **Berengaria**

Hotels without star/guest houses
Alps, Overhill

Pedhoulas
3-star
Churchill Pinewood Valley
2-star **Marangos**
1-star **Central**

Hotels without star/guest houses
Christy's Palace, Elyssia, Jack's Place, Kallithea, Koundouris

Kalopanayiotis
Hotels without star/guest houses
Drakos, Helioupolis, Kastalia, Loutraki, Synnos

Kakopetria
3-star **Makris**
2-star **Hekali, Hellas**
1-star **Krystal**

Hotels without star/guest houses
Kifissia, Loukoudi

Galata
1-star **Rialto**

Perapedhi
Hotels without star/guest houses
Paradisos, Pera Pedhi

Agros
Hotels without star/guest houses
Meteora

Kyperounda
Hotels without star/guest houses
Livadhia

Other tourist facilities run by the Cyprus Tourism Organisation

Tourist beaches
Dassoudi
(3m. east of Limassol)
Larnaca Beach
(6m. east of Larnaca)
Yeroskipos Beach
(2m. east of Paphos)

Tourist pavilions
Troodos Resort
Baths of Aphrodite
Curium
Petra tou Romiou
Tekke of Umm Haram

Exploring Cyprus

Petra tou Romiou (Aphrodite's Bay)

For the traveller with a car, Cyprus offers endless possibilities of exploring history. Not merely Cypriot history, but the history of Europe and Western Asia, condensed into a small area of 3,572 square miles. Art and superstition, religious achievement and commercial adventurism, military might and pastoral tranquillity are all recorded in the stones laid by man since the first settlements of the Stone Age, nearly 8,000 years ago.

But a search for the island's history offers more than the thrill and enlightenment of the eventual discovery. It offers the adventure of getting there, driving through scenery that varies from the vine and forest-clad mountains of Troodos to the bare plain of the Mesaoria, and over roads that vary from the fast highways into the Troodos from north and south to the unmade tracks that are no more than a crooked hairline on the map. But in an island as small as Cyprus, and with such good communications, no journey can seem too arduous, particularly when it offers such rewards.

First in historical order are the **Neolithic sites**. The best preserved of these is at **Khirokitia**, a short drive along the coast road from Limassol. This is the record, in layers of stone and mud brick (now restored and reinforced) of the island's first settlers, who built their homes here in 5800 BC. Perhaps the most remarkable of all archaeological discoveries in Cyprus were made in these huts, the beehive-shaped *tholoi*. Digging through successive layers of earth, the excavators found the skeletons of the people who had been interred, generation after generation, beneath the floors of the huts, with the innumerable household objects that had been buried with them. From these remains much was learned about the Stone Age people: their architecture, their implements, their way of life. To see these relics, and those of later sites, the visitor is recommended to go to the Cyprus Museum in Nicosia, which houses one of the finest archaeological collections in the Levant.

The **Bronze Age** in Cyprus is best represented by the ancient city of *Enkomi/Alasia, five miles north of Famagusta. This city, revealed to the world by Professor C. F. A. Schaeffer in 1934, marks an important epoch in Cypriot history (*c.*1500 BC) when the island had achieved, through the mining and export of copper, a commercial status that made it the focus of attention for the rival powers of the Eastern Mediterranean. After a series of earthquakes in the 11th c. BC it gave way to the nearby Salamis.

Of the early period of **Greek colonisation**, which began in 1400 BC and which ethnically had the greatest impact on the character of the Cypriot people, little trace remains. Earthquakes and pirate raids have done much to bury the Greek past: the ancient city kingdoms that provided the island's first civilisation based on a common religion, language and democratic system. The vestiges of Greek architecture that exist belong to a later period, when the island was being commercially developed by the trading nations of the Middle East. The most dramatic reminder of the Persian period of influence is the Palace of **Vouni**, standing on a headland overlooking the Bay of Morphou. This palace, built by the pro-Persian king of Marion in the 5th c. BC, was destroyed by fire in 380 BC. Although the Swedish team who discovered the palace in 1928 were able to uncover little more than the foundations, the stones have been permanently preserved *in situ* by setting them in concrete (the method used at Khirokitia).

The sea was never far from the gaze of the Greeks, as can be seen from the siting of their two most important temples: the **Temple of Apollo** at **Curium**

and the **Temple of Aphrodite** at **Palea Paphos**. When the Greeks moved inland, they did so for a purpose. **Idalion** and **Tamassos** offered the spoils of copper, long to be associated with the prosperity of the island. The settlements have disappeared, but at Tamassos, an ancient city-kingdom south-east of Nicosia, excavations have revealed two royal tombs dating from the 6th c. BC. From approximately the same period are the **Tombs of the Kings** in the royal necropolis at*Salamis, on the road to St Barnabas Monastery. These tombs, excavated in 1962, revealed some interesting details of the ritual of a royal burial, in which the possessions of the deceased — ranging from pottery to the king's personal chariot and horse team — were interred at the same time, usually in the entrance passage to the burial chamber.

Of the many ancient tombs discovered in Cyprus the most spectacular, belonging to the **Hellenistic** period, are the so-called **Tombs of the Kings** at **Paphos** (3rd c. BC). These tombs, located on a bare, deserted stretch of the shore north of the site of Nea Paphos, hold their mystery for all who visit them, whether the casual sightseer or the archaeologist. The approach arouses curiosity, whets suspense: an empty road ruled straight across a scrub-covered plain to no apparent objective, finishing suddenly on a plateau of rock overlooking the sea. The tombs, cut out of the rock, are not immediately visible, and one wonders what one has come to see. Then, unexpectedly, a cavern opens in the ground and steps lead down to a court, open to the sky and framed by a graceful colonnade. Behind these columns — like the rest of the court, cut out of the rock — lie the entrances to the burial chambers, now empty. About a hundred tombs, of varying size and complexity, honeycomb the area, all carved laboriously from the rock. The mystery of their name remains. Built for eternity, but at a date which unfortunately makes it impossible for any Cypriot king to have been entombed in them.

Also at **Nea Paphos**, two miles from the tombs, is the most exciting discovery made in Cyprus since the war. Here lies a superb memorial to the **Roman** era, the extensive villa known as the **House of Dionysos**, built in the 3rd c. AD. The ploughshare that accidentally uncovered part of a mosaic pavement in 1962 was the beginning of a series of excavations that finally revealed a total of 22 rooms, 14 of them with mosaic floors representing scenes of hunting and mythology. The identity of the rich Roman has not been declared: it is tempting to think of him as the governor of the Roman province of Cyprus, whose chief city was Paphos.

The visitor in search of Roman Cyprus will find it in her two most important sites: **Curium** and*Salamis. Originally city-kingdoms of the Greeks, they were largely rebuilt by the Romans. Both are wonderfully situated: Curium on a towering headland overlooking the sea to the west of Limassol; Salamis on the east coast, north of Famagusta, its ruins lost in a scented forest of mimosa and eucalyptus. And for the student of the past, both hold a particular fascination. They are still, in the archaeological sense, growing cities. Since the island's independence there has been a consistent programme of excavation at both sites, carried out by teams from French and American universities and by the Cyprus Department of Antiquities. To enjoy a comprehensive view of the sites, the visitor should allow sufficient time: half a day at least for Curium, a whole day for Salamis.

Another city kingdom currently under excavation is **Amathus**, on the south coast near Limassol. Here the outline of the city walls, the acropolis and part of the lower city have been revealed.

Mosaics at House of Dionysos, Paphos   33

The most recent discovery at Salamis, a basilica of the 4th c. AD, marks the transition of the pagan Cyprus to the Cyprus of early Christianity. The city, destroyed by an earthquake, was rebuilt as Constantia, in honour of the Roman Emperor Constantius II. It was his predecessor, Constantine the Great, who had officially recognised the Christian Church and moved the capital of the Roman Empire from Rome to Byzantium. The end of the century saw the beginning of the **Byzantine Empire**, and of the development of the church architecture and decoration to which Cyprus owes her artistic tradition.

Byzantine art in Cyprus can be looked at in three phases. The first belongs to the period of the early Christian churches (4th–7th c. AD). These were built in the style of the timber-roofed Roman basilica and decorated in a similar manner, with mosaic floors and murals. The best examples of these basilica churches are found in the ruins of **Salamis (Constantia), Peyia** near Paphos and the village of **Kato Paphos**, all of which have vestiges of mosaic floors. The only two churches with wall mosaics of the period are at **Kiti** (Panagia Angeloktistos) and ·**Lythrangomi** (Panagia Kanakaria). It must be noted here that the existing churches are of a later date than their apses, which contain the mosaics. These apses are survivals from the earlier basilica churches, destroyed by the Arabs in the 7th c. AD. The mosaic at Kiti, which is near the salt lake south-west of Larnaca, is worth a special journey. It shows the *Virgin Mary and Child attended by Archangels*, a beautiful composition which has a special significance in Byzantine art, belonging to the period before the iconoclastic movement in Byzantium in which all representations of religious figures – in mosaic or other form – were destroyed.

For three and a half centuries, while the Arab invasions continued, there was little development of church art or architecture in Cyprus. But in the 10th c. the Byzantine Empire re-asserted itself as the dominant power in the Eastern Mediterranean and the next two centuries – the golden age of Byzantine art – saw the greatest achievement of Cypriot ecclesiastical art.

The style of church architecture followed that of the Byzantine capital, Constantinople, with the dome as a central theme and the body of the church either single-aisled, with a vault, or cross-shaped. The symbolism of church decoration was also in the Byzantine tradition, with the Christ Pantocrator in the dome representing God in heaven, the New Testament cycle on the walls (God on earth), and the Virgin Mary, usually with the Infant Jesus, in the semi-dome of the apse (Incarnation).

Where Cypriot decoration differed from that of Constantinople was in its emphasis on wall painting. This was much less costly than mosaic work and was commonly employed throughout the island, in monasteries and small village churches alike. The artists came from different parts of the Empire – mainly the capital – and their work shows interesting variations of style, most notably the contrast between the natural, neo-classical approach to figure-drawing and the harder, more linear 'monastic' style. The high point of their achievement – in the 12th and 13th c. – can be viewed in churches scattered across the breadth of the island.

Apart from their paintings these churches have in common an alluring remoteness which enhances the pleasure of visiting them. The finest, without doubt, is the Church of Panagia Phorbiotissa at **Asinou**, which now, with the development of the Nicosia-Troodos highway, is one of the more accessible. An eight-mile drive along a road branching off the highway 22 miles west of

Nicosia leads, via the village of Nikitari, to the little church which is a leading monument of Byzantine art, with paintings dating from the early 12th c. to the late 15th c.

An important point must be made here to all those intending to visit Cyprus' painted churches. Because of their remoteness the majority of them do not have a priest in attendance and are kept locked. It is important therefore to always ask in the village for the key (in Greek, *to kleethi*) in the local café, which will usually result in the visitor being directed to the house of the priest or being offered the services of a guide, who can be anyone from a schoolboy to an octogenerian but who will be unfailingly helpful. In the case of Asinou, the priest will be found in the village of Nikitari, three miles from the church, and will happily accompany visitors in their car.

In all there are about two dozen historic painted churches in Cyprus, all worth a visit. But for the average traveller on a two or three-week trip this would be an extreme, if not impossible luxury. Special mention is therefore reserved for three, apart from Asinou, which should not be missed. Two are in the Troodos region, at **Lagoudhera** and **Kakopetria**. The Church of Panagia tou Arakou at Lagoudhera, in the district of Pitsilia, has paintings recently restored by the Institute of Byzantine Studies at Dumbarton Oaks (Harvard) which represent the most comprehensive series of a single period (late 12th c.) in the island. The 12th c. Church of Ayios Nicolaos tis Steyis, situated on the side of a beautiful wooded valley three miles from Kakopetria by asphalt road, is easier to reach but no less rewarding. Apart from history these two churches have in common a typical feature of the mountain churches of Cyprus: a steep-pitched, tiled roof. In the case of both churches these roofs were added over the existing domed roof as a protection against weather: in later churches they were an integral part of the building.

Another painted church that is in reality a cave sanctuary, is the **Encleistra** of the hermit St Neophyte, situated six miles north of Paphos next to the monastery that bears his name **(Ayios Neophytos)**. This tiny refuge, hollowed out by the hermit's own hands, consists of three consecutive caves, all painted during his lifetime (late 12th c.) with scenes from the New Testament. It is a miniature gallery of Byzantine art in its most interesting period, when the monastic and neo-classical styles were in conflict. The paintings are very beautiful, covering the whole area of the rock.

The last phase of Cypro-Byzantine art belongs to the period when Cyprus was no longer part of Byzantium but under Latin rule, and when the Empire itself was in ruins after the conquests of the Turks. Fugitives from Constantinople and other parts of the broken Empire came to Cyprus and there followed, in the mid-15th c., a great revival of Byzantine art in the island: church building, wall-decoration, icon painting. This is now identified as the post-Byzantine local revival style and is best seen in the Church of Stavros tou Agiasmati at **Platanistasa**. At the same time, in response to the Italian Renaissance, there was a development of the Italo-Byzantine style, influenced by the fresco painters of Florence. The distrust between the Greek Orthodox and Latin Churches was such, however, that the style was not commonly adopted in the island. The best example of Italo-Byzantine work is in the Latin Chapel of the Monastery of St John Lampadistis in **Kalopanayiotis**.

Apart from the painted churches the most impressive relics of the Byzantine period are without doubt the three castles on the Kyrenia range, ***St Hilarion,*Buffavento** and***Kantara**. Originally part of the system of fortifications built to protect the island from the Arab raiders, the castles were enlarged and refortified in the Lusignan period and are now commonly referred to as 'Crusader castles'. Although the Venetians dismantled the castles in the 16th c., there are substantial ruins of both Byzantine and Lusignan periods which make intriguing exploration. From below, perched on their dizzy crags, the abandoned strongholds seem dauntingly remote.

The three hundred years of **Lusignan** rule are best recalled by the beautiful churches, built in the French Gothic style, that the Frankish princes endowed with their riches. The island's grandest monuments of medieval architecture are the *Cathedral of St Sophia in Nicosia and the *Cathedral of St Nicholas in Famagusta, both completed in the 14th c. After the Turkish conquest of the island in 1571 these Latin cathedrals were both converted into mosques for the practice of the Muslim faith. They are now the principal places of worship for the Turkish-Cypriot minority, situated in the Turkish quarters of the two cities. Happily, their conversion has done no more than the ravages of time to alter their character, and their architecture remains an outstanding memorial to the soldiers of the Cross who for three centuries tried to recover the Holy Land for Christendom, and to establish the Latin Church in the Eastern Mediterranean.

There are many other Latin churches in Cyprus, but most of them are in Nicosia and Famagusta. Within the walls of the old city of Famagusta it is believed that there were once as many as 365 churches, and there are

View from Kolossi Castle

sufficient remains for the visitor to be able to reconstruct the medieval city in a walking tour, to gain some impression from those hollow, Gothic shapes of its former splendour. Outside the cities, the chief foundation of the rulers of Latin Cyprus was the Abbey of *Bellapais (13th–14th c.) the island's most beautiful monastic building.

No reference to the monuments of the Lusignan period can omit **Kolossi Castle**. The fortified keep, standing like a square yellow block on the bare landscape of the plain west of Limassol, was built by the Knights of St John of Jerusalem, who were granted estates here by the Lusignan King Hugh I as a reward for their services in the Crusades. The battlements of the castle afford a striking view of the terrain which served the Commandery and made it the Knights' wealthiest overseas possession. The sugar plantations have gone, but the vineyards still flourish, stretching away to the foothills of the Troodos.

During the **Venetian** period the emphasis of architecture was on fortification. The record of this is in the massive walls that now surround the old cities of **Nicosia** and *Famagusta** and in the majestic stronghold of *Kyrenia Castle**. In each case, existing Lusignan buildings had to be destroyed or reinforced to create the new defences, which were designed to withstand the bombardment of heavy cannon. The severest loss to Lusignan architecture was in Nicosia, where the Venetians reduced the circumference of the original city — six miles — by half and destroyed all buildings outside the new walls

that obstructed the field of fire. In the 20th c. adaptations to the city, history has, in a sense, repeated itself. In many places the walls have been levelled off and new openings created — so as not to obstruct the flow of modern traffic. In contrast to Nicosia, the walls of Famagusta have preserved their original character and are without doubt the finest example of 16th c. Venetian military architecture. One of the greatest pleasures for the unhurried visitor to Famagusta is a walking tour of the walls, a circuit of less than two miles that provides a close-up view of the towering ramparts and bastions of this great fortress-city.

With their energies concentrated on defence, there was little new church architecture carried out by the Venetians during their occupation. One example, however, suggests a pleasant excursion for all visitors to Famagusta. This is the Monastery of **Ayia Napa**, situated at the edge of a fishing village of the same name nine miles south of Famagusta. This monastery, which possesses a beautiful octagonal fountain, is perfectly situated on a gentle crest over-looking the sea, within sight of the fishing boats in the little rock-girt harbour.

The three centuries of **Turkish** rule left one distinct mark on the island's architecture: the pencil-shaped minarets of the mosques. Many of the mosques were not, however, Turkish-built but created by the conversion of Christian churches. The purely Turkish architecture is mainly domestic, although there are some good examples of the traditional *khan* (Turkish inn) in Nicosia. The most important Turkish monument in Cyprus is the **Tekke of Umm Haram** (Hala Sultan Tekke) which reputedly contains the relics of the foster-mother (or aunt?) of the Prophet Mohammed. This exalted Arab lady, while travelling with her husband on an expedition across Cyprus in the 7th c. AD, had the misfortune to fall from her mule and break her neck, at a spot near the salt lake south-west of **Larnaca** where her tomb now stands, in an 18th c. mosque. Driving out to the silver-white expanse of the salt lake, where the shrine appears like a distant mirage in its oasis clump of pine and cypress, one can imagine oneself a part of that fateful expedition 1,300 years ago that was to leave its mark so indelibly on this corner of the Muslim world.

No description of the explorer's Cyprus would be complete without a mention of her most remote, but keenly-sought pleasures: the **monasteries**. Most were founded in the early years of Christianity, usually as an act of dedication by a group of hermits who, coming into possession of a holy relic or icon, would build a church — and subsequently a monastery — to contain and protect it. The early buildings have now disappeared, largely as the result of fire, but the sacred treasures — and the spirit that created their guardian churches — survives. The most important monastery, **Kykko**, is in the wildest and least explored part of the island on the west side of the Troodos. A visit there must be the climax to any holiday in Cyprus — if this is measured by a view of unending pine-clad mountains, the friendliness of a monk whose time belongs to his visitor, or a sip of that fragrant rose-flavoured drink that is part of the welcome.

The pleasure of the visit can be prolonged by overnight accommodation — offered without charge and with appropriate simplicity at most of the monasteries. The only exception to this is **Stavrovouni**, which does not offer accommodation to women. An unfortunate exception, as anyone who can drive up that spiral staircase road to reach the 2,258' eyrie with its three monks, unnumbered cats and breath-taking view of south-eastern Cyprus, deserves a rest!

Using the guide

The maps on this and the following pages show recommended itineraries for motoring excursions in Cyprus. The centres chosen are at different points of the island and offer the best facilities for tourists: accommodation, restaurants and entertainment. They are **Larnaca**, **Nicosia**, **Limassol** and **Paphos**.

Most of the excursions are of one-day duration, allowing time for the return journey. Some of those which include the Troodos, however, allow for an overnight stay in the mountains. For those who have only a brief period in the island and do not wish to do all the tours, a choice may be made among them (see opposite page).

The itinerary maps can also be used by tourists who plan a less strenuous holiday, i.e. those who are staying at one centre for their entire holiday and are only making occasional excursions. If, for example, you are spending your holiday in Paphos, the relevant map will show you all the interesting places to visit in this part of the island. By varying their centres tourists will, of course, give themselves greater manoeuvrability and greater coverage of the island, but Cyprus is small enough not to impose limitations even on those who are staying at one centre. It is quite possible, for example, to drive from Nicosia to Paphos via Limassol in three hours.

The Gazetteer section which follows the maps is intended as a handy reference for visitors seeking a brief history or description of the places visited on the excursions.

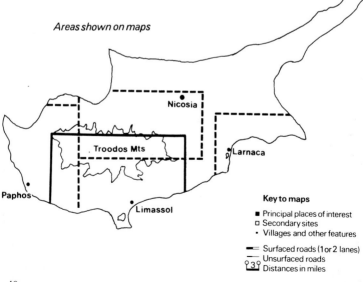

Areas shown on maps

Nicosia

Troodos Mts

Larnaca

Paphos

Limassol

Key to maps

■ Principal places of interest
□ Secondary sites
· Villages and other features

▬ Surfaced roads (1 or 2 lanes)
— Unsurfaced roads
〇3〇 Distances in miles

Road maps and itineraries

THE ROAD MAPS

All places listed in the Gazetteer are shown on
the maps. Those not included in the excursions
as primary attractions or purely for the purposes
of direction are in lighter type.
As these maps show only the main network of
roads it is suggested that they are used in
conjunction with an ordnance survey map of
the island (see p. 21)

THE ITINERARIES

Excursions are suitable for one day unless
otherwise stated. Return routes are the same as
outgoing routes unless otherwise stated.
The excursions shown in bold type are
recommended for those who wish to see
the most important sites. Other excursions
are shown in lighter type.

Mileages shown on map

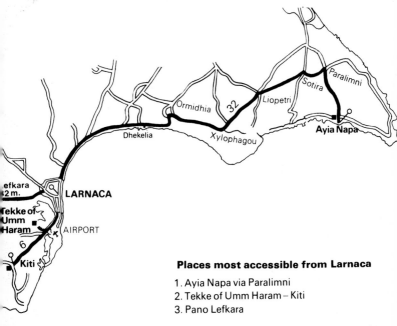

Places most accessible from Larnaca

1. Ayia Napa via Paralimni
2. Tekke of Umm Haram – Kiti
3. Pano Lefkara

Places most accessible from Nicosia

*4. **Pedhoulas via Peristerona, Amiandos and Mt Olympus – Moutoullas – Kalopanayiotis – Troodhitissa – Platres** (return via Amiandos)
Alternative to Excursion 10

5. Peristerona – Asinou – Galata – Kakopetria

6. Tamassos – Makheras

*7. The Pitsilia region (Palekhori, Lagoudhera, Platanistasa) via Pano Dheftera (return via Peristerona)

8. Perakhorio – Pyrga – *Stavrovouni

*Indicates outstanding scenery

Mileages shown on map

Key to map

■ Principal places of interest
□ Secondary sites
· Villages and other features

══ Surfaced roads (1 or 2 lanes)
── Unsurfaced roads
⌐3⌐ Distances in miles

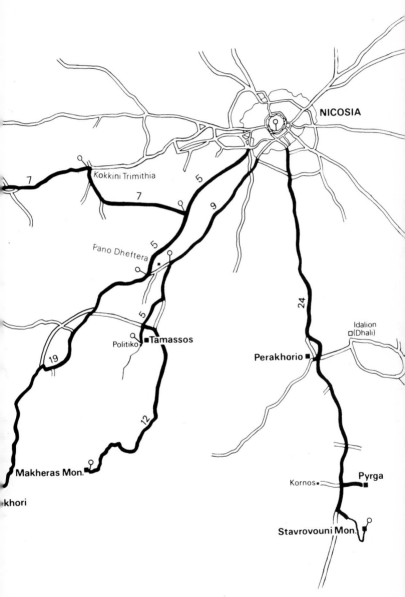

NICOSIA

7

Kokkini Trimithia

7

5

9

Pano Dheftera

5

5

19

Politiko ■ Tamassos

12

Makheras Mon. ■

khori

24

Idalion
□ (Dhali)

Perakhorio ■

Kornos ■ Pyrga ■

Stavrovouni Mon. ■

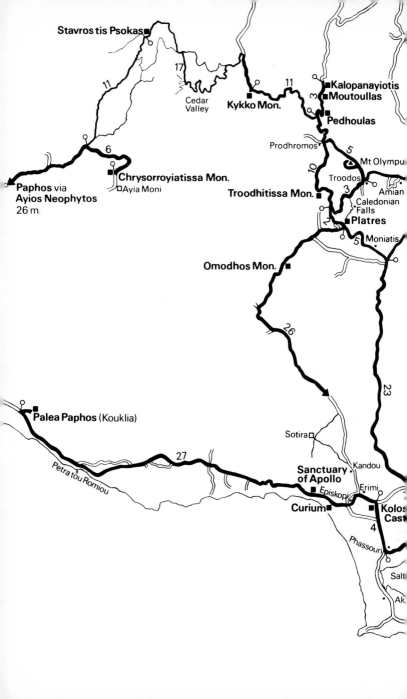

Places most accessible from Limassol

9. **Kolossi via Phassouri – Curium and Sanctuary of Apollo – Palea Paphos (Kouklia) via *Petra tou Romiou** (visitors staying in Paphos (Ktima) may prefer to visit Palea Paphos from here (see Excursion 15))

*10. **Pedhoulas via Amiandos and Mt Olympus – Moutoullas – Kalopanayiotis – Troodhitissa – Platres – Omodhos** (return to Limassol via Kandou)
Alternative to Excursion 4

*11. **Platres via Moniatis – Pedhoulas via Mt Olympus – Moutoullas – Kalopanayiotis – Kykko – Stavros – Chrysorroyiatissa – Ayios Neophytos – Paphos** (overnight stay at Kykko or Stavros, return from Paphos to Limassol via coast road)
Alternative to Excursions 4, 10 & 13
Khirokitia via Amathus – Pano Lefkara

* Indicates outstanding scenery
Mileages shown on map

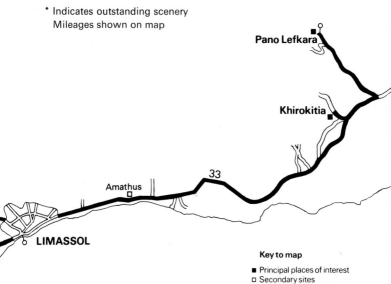

Key to map

■ Principal places of interest
□ Secondary sites
• Villages and other features

━ Surfaced roads (1 or 2 lanes)
— Unsurfaced roads
<u>39</u> Distances in miles

45

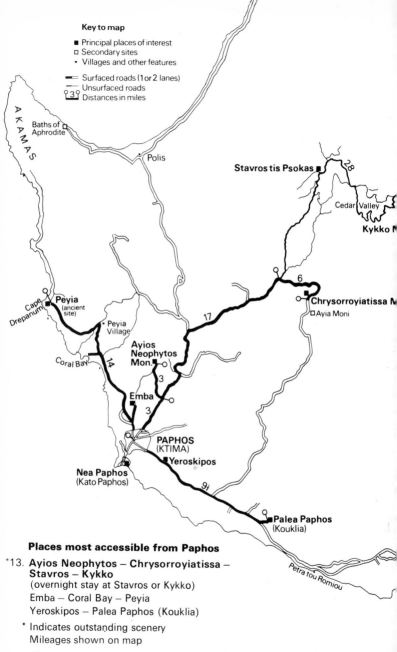

Key to map

- ■ Principal places of interest
- □ Secondary sites
- • Villages and other features

Surfaced roads (1 or 2 lanes)
Unsurfaced roads
3 Distances in miles

AKAMAS

Baths of Aphrodite

Polis

Stavros tis Psokas ■ 28

Cedar Valley

Kykko M

6

Chrysorroyiatissa M

□ Ayia Moni

17

Cape Drepanum ■ Peyia (ancient site)

• Peyia Village

Coral Bay

14

Ayios Neophytos Mon. ■

3

Emba ■

3

PAPHOS (KTIMA)

Nea Paphos (Kato Paphos)

■ Yeroskipos

9½

■ Palea Paphos (Kouklia)

Petra tou Romiou

Places most accessible from Paphos

*13. **Ayios Neophytos – Chrysorroyiatissa – Stavros – Kykko**
  (overnight stay at Stavros or Kykko)
  Emba – Coral Bay – Peyia
  Yeroskipos – Palea Paphos (Kouklia)

  * Indicates outstanding scenery
  Mileages shown on map

Makheras Monastery

This Gazetteer contains information on the location, history and main features of the places of interest in Cyprus. Information about hotels, restaurants etc. will be found in the Practical Information section.

Many place names in Cyprus have two or more forms. The policy of this guide is to use the form most commonly recognised by English-speaking visitors: e.g. the Latin 'Curium' in preference to the Greek 'Kourion'. It should be noted that the Greek word for 'Saint' is 'Ayios' or 'Ayia'.

Altitudes shown (2,000' or more) are approximate.

Details of entrance fees and opening hours of museums and ancient monuments are on p. 28.

* The asterisk indicates places in the northern area of the island occupied by the Turkish army and subject to the limitations of access detailed on p.20. The information on these places has not been updated since the first edition of this guide (1972)

Agros (3,200') Village in the Pitsilia region of the Troodos. A summer resort, with modest accommodation, in the midst of attractive mountain scenery. To the south of Agros lies the region where the famous dessert wine *Commandaria* is produced.

Akamas The north-western peninsula of Cyprus, a wild uninhabited region. A dirt road leads from Cape Drepanum to Cape Arnauti at the tip of the peninsula (18m.)

Akrotiri The south-western peninsula of Cyprus, a flat expanse largely occupied by a salt lake where a great variety of bird migrants can be seen at different times of the year. To the south of the lake is the British air base, the largest RAF station overseas. Access to the base is limited to service personnel and their families.

Amathus One of the ancient city kingdoms of Cyprus, situated on the south coast 5½m. east of Limassol. Although this was probably a Mycenaean settlement, like the other city kingdoms, no archaeological evidence of Mycenaean occupation has yet been uncovered. Such evidence may result, however, from the current programme of excavations.

The importance of Amathus lay in its port, from which it exported copper and timber. Its relationship with the other city kingdoms was ambivalent. During the revolt of the Greek states of Asia Minor against their Persian overlords (Ionian Revolt, 499 BC), the city sided with the Persians, and it was in a battle near here that the Greek hero Onesilos of Salamis was killed by the Amathusians.

The city's prosperity continued in Hellenistic and Roman times, the main periods exposed by recent excavations. Much of the city was destroyed by earthquakes in the 4th c. AD, but it recovered, only to suffer from Arab raids in the 7th-8th c. When Richard the Lionheart landed here in 1191 prior to his conquest of the island, it is probable that the city had been abandoned. The ruins of the ancient city were subsequently pillaged for building purposes, the major shipment of stones going to Egypt for the construction of the Suez Canal. The American Consul di Cesnola carried out his own 'excavations', removing many antiquities to America. Despite these ravages there is still undoubtedly a wealth of material to be uncovered in this extensive site.

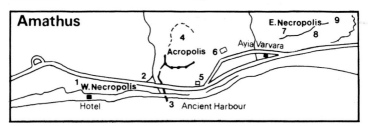

Amathus

Asinou Church

Tour The site of ancient Amathus, consisting of the acropolis, lower city and necropolis areas, extends along 2m. of coastline, eastwards from the Amathus Beach Hotel. The most obvious feature is the large number of tombs, either built or rock-cut, which are to be found either to the east or the west of the city.

In the **western necropolis**, the most impressive is the underground *built tomb* (7th c. BC) **(1)** in the garden of the Amathus Beach Hotel. This has a stepped passage (*dromos*) leading down to the burial chamber. Other built tombs can be seen on the opposite side of the road and further on, on the same side, but many of these have been obscured by building development.

Proceeding eastwards, one shortly reaches an open area on the left with two lime kilns. Behind these is a *rock-cut tomb* **(2)** entered at ground level, with three burial chambers. Crossing a river valley one then reaches the line of the western wall of the city, with its *promontory* **(3)** jutting out over the sea. To the east of this jutting fragment lay the ancient harbour of Amathus.

The line of the wall from this point to the acropolis has disappeared, but much of the southern part of the **enceinte** of the Romano-Byzantine city has survived: the lower cladding of dressed stone and the rubble infill to a greater height. Following the line of this wall around the acropolis hill one can see the southern gate and the bases of regularly-placed towers. At the top of the hill is a complex of buildings around a *Temple of Aphrodite* **(4)**, which can be located by the remains of a huge stone jar at its entrance.

At the foot of the acropolis hill, by the main road, is an early Christian *basilica* (5th–7th c. AD) **(5)** with three aisles and an adjoining chapel, presenting a fourth apse on the south side.

The depression between the acropolis hill and the hill of the eastern necropolis is the scene of the most recent archaeological activity (Dept. of Antiquities). This is the site of the **lower city**, and excavations have revealed **(6)** a section of the Romano-Byzantine *agora*, with an impressive array of architectural fragments that are witness to the force of the earthquakes which ravaged the city in the 4th c. AD.

By the church of Ayia Varvara, at the end of the slip road, one ascends the hill of the **eastern necropolis**. In an enclosure north-east of the church are a number of *built tombs* **(7)**: further on, in the rocky slope below the path, is a honeycomb of *rock-cut tombs* **(8)**. At the easternmost point of the hill are two huge rock-cut *water cisterns*, one of them converted into the shrine of *Ayia Varvara*, with an adjacent early Christian *basilica* **(9)** used for the city's burial ceremonies.

Amiandos (4,500′) An asbestos mine, 5m. from Troodos resort, which takes its name from two nearby villages (Pano Amiandos and Kato Amiandos). The mine, which was opened in 1907, is expected to continue in use for another 100 years. The vast grey amphitheatre of crushed rock that marks the mine presents a spectacular sight from the mountain road.

Antiphonitis The Byzantine **Church of Christ Antiphonitis** stands in romantic isolation in a corner of the Kyrenia range, east of the Pentadactylos mountain. There is usually a custodian in attendance, but if the church is locked the key may be obtained at the nearby village of Ayios Amvrosios. Once part of a disused monastery, the church was built in the 12th c. Its style is unusual, with a single aisle and a disproportionately large dome. The narthex at the west end of the church was added by the Lusignans in the 15th c. A further addition, from the same period, was the elegant Gothic loggia to the south, which once supported a flat wooden roof. Inside, the church is dominated by the dome, carried on squinches supported by eight columns. The unevenness of the construction and the imperfect circle of the dome suggest that local workmen were employed, and the wall-painters who followed them had obvious difficulties in adapting their compositions to the irregular proportions

of the church. The paintings in the bema and the south-west corner of the nave (note particularly the *Baptism of Christ*) are from the 12th c.; the remainder from the 15th. Of these the most impressive are the *Tree of Jesse* on the north wall below the dome and the *Last Judgement* on the south.

* **Aphendrika** A Byzantine site, with pre-Christian vestiges, in the north-eastern end of the Karpas. It has yet to be fully excavated.

* **Apostolos Andreas Monastery**, at the end of the Karpas peninsula, is the furthest point that can be reached on the main road. It is not in fact a monastery but a hostel for Greek Orthodox pilgrims who hold this as a sacred spot. It was here that St Andrew is supposed to have put in for water, during a return voyage to Palestine. The water, with which the saint effected a miraculous cure, is believed to have come from a well near the seashore, now enclosed by a **chapel**. This chapel is of the 15th c., but the church and the buildings of the hostel are modern. The most popular days of pilgrimage are August 15th (Assumption) and November 30th (Saint's day). The pilgrims bring with them offerings, including wax effigies (for the cure of afflictions) which can be seen in the church.

Asinou The **Church of Panagia Phorbiotissa** at Asinou is acknowledged as the finest example of the painted church in Cyprus. The frescoes, which have recently been cleaned, present a clear and detailed record of the development of Byzantine and post-Byzantine art in the island from the beginning of the 12th c., when the church was built, to the end of the 15th c. The church is situated 3 m. from Nikitari, a village north-east of Troodos, on the site of an ancient city (Assinou or Asine) founded by Greeks in the 11th c. BC. The priest, who lives in Nikitari, will accompany visitors with the key.

Externally the church is unimpressive, and small even by comparison with other Byzantine churches in Cyprus. The structure is simple: a barrel-vaulted nave backed by a domed narthex, the whole covered by a protective steep-pitched roof. Internally it is a revelation of colour and beauty, with every surface covered by vivid and passionate paintings. The earliest work, belonging to the first period of building (1106) is to be seen in the apse and the western part of the nave. The *Communion of the Apostles* in the apse is to be specially admired for its study of Christ offering the wine to John (note the manner in which Christ gazes after the departing Judas). Over the west door of the nave is the *Dormition of the Virgin Mary* showing Christ holding his mother's soul as a swaddled infant. On either side of the door, and in the south-west recess, are paintings of saints, and in the north-west recess the paintings of the *Forty Martyrs of Saint Sebasto*, standing in a frozen lake with blood pouring from their wounds. A painting from the same period, but restored in the 15th c., is of the donor of the church *Nicephorus Magistros* over the south door. He is here shown presenting a model of the church to Christ, with the Virgin Mary looking on. The paintings in the narthex are of the 14th c., with the *Last Judgement* as the central theme. In the cupola *Christ the Judge* looks down, surrounded by angels and with the twelve Apostles portrayed on the pendentives. On the arches supporting the cupola are a succession of *Saints* (north arch) and *Sinners* (south arch). In the north apse of the narthex is an interesting representation of the *Land* and the *Sea*; opposite, in the south apse, a mounted *St George*. The remainder of

West door, Asinou

the church, including the vault of the nave, was largely painted in the late 15th c. The less formal approach of the post-Byzantine period, when local artists were employed, provides an interesting comparison with the work of four centuries earlier.

Ayia Irini Village north of Morphou, 1 m. from Morphou Bay. Site of the discovery, in a sacred enclosure of the 6th–7th c. BC, of the remarkable collection of terracotta figures now in the Cyprus Museum.

Ayia Moni Monastery (3,700′), now disused, is 2 m. from the larger monastery of Chrysorroyiatissa, in the Paphos district. Founded in the 6th c., the **church** retains an apse from this period. The rest is a 17th c. reconstruction. Set in its rustic courtyard, and with its looming mountain backdrop, the church has a special charm and is worth a diversion.

Ayia Napa Monastery stands at the foot of a small fishing village of that name, 9 m. south of Famagusta. Attractively sited, within a short distance of the

sea, this monastery was built in the 16th c. by the Venetians, shortly before the Turkish conquest. It is perfectly preserved: a fascinating echo of the Republic in a far-flung corner of its influence.

The monastery, enclosed by a high wall, is entered by a gateway on the north side. On the right is a large two-storied gatehouse, which creates the impression of a fortification. By contrast, in the centre of the courtyard, is a beautiful octagonal **fountain**, sculptured in high relief on each side with garlands, animals' heads and coats-of-arms. The fountain is shaded by a dome resting on four pillars. A second fountain, in the form of an ornamental boar's head, is on the north

Fountain, Ayia Napa

side of the courtyard. The **church**, which is partly underground, is entered by a flight of steps. Converted to Greek Orthodox use after the Turkish conquest, it retains a Latin chapel.

Ayios Chrysostomos Monastery 8 m. north of Nicosia, on the way to Buffavento Castle in the Kyrenia range. Traditionally founded by the Empress Helena, the monastery is now largely modern and at present occupied by a military garrison. Access is however permitted to its most interesting feature, the **double church** that is entered from the south. The first half of the building (1891) replaces the original Church of Ayios Chrysostomos, and contains a few relics of its predecessor: the floor of the apse, some icons, and a fine wooden west door, made up of geometrically-carved pieces that have been fitted together without nails. The church to the north (Holy Trinity) belongs to the 11th–12th c., with frescoes of the period which although fragmentary have been recently restored with great skill by the Dumbarton Oaks Byzantine Institute, U.S.A.

Ayios Neophytos Monastery 6 m. north of Paphos, commemorates the extraordinary life of St Neophyte the Recluse (born 1134), a monk who after seven years at the Monastery of Ayios Chrysostomos, near Nicosia, decided to become a hermit and came to this remote valley in search of a retreat. For a year he laboured to excavate a cave in the hillside, incorporating a chapel, a sanctuary and a private room. Later, to seek further seclusion, he retreated to another cave, further up the hillside. His total period of seclusion, up to his death, was about 60 years. St Neophyte's devout withdrawal from the world had, however, the opposite effect to that intended. His disciples grew so great in number that a community formed around him, the beginning of the monastery that exists today. The church of the monastery now contains the saint's remains, removed in 1750 from the tomb in the cell of his cave.

Beyond the monastery the **Encleistra** (refuge of the saint) can be reached by a flight of steps ascending the rockface. The three chambers of the cave are all beautifully painted, much of the work carried out under the direction of the saint himself. In the nave of the chapel, entered first, the compositions progress through the drama of Calvary to the *Ascension* in the dome-shaped ceiling. Most of these compositions belong to the 12th c., the time of St Neophyte. In the adjoining sanctuary the saint can be seen portrayed on the ceiling, conveyed to heaven by two archangels. On either side of the door connecting the sanctuary to the cell is a poetic *Annunciation*, and on the ceiling above the altar a second composition of the *Ascension* that has been skilfully adapted to the uneven surface of the rock. The last chamber, a tiny cell measuring only 11'×8', contains the saint's bed — a carved recess in the rock — and a table and seat, also cut out of the rock. The paintings in this cell include a *Resurrection* depicting St Neophyte at the feet of Christ, and two further studies of the *Crucifixion*, emphasising the saint's dedication of his refuge to the Holy Cross.

Baths of Aphrodite Beauty spot 6 m. west of Polis, by legend the bathing place of the Goddess of Love. A footpath leads from the tourist pavilion to a grotto with a pool fed by a perennial spring, in the midst of a dense growth of bamboo and fern.

***Bellapais** Village $3\frac{1}{2}$ m. east of Kyrenia, which takes its name from the beautiful **abbey**, founded at the end of the 12th c., which is one of the great monuments of Gothic architecture in the Levant. The siting of the village on the lower slopes of the Kyrenia range, with the fortified mass of the abbey making a forward barbican on the seaward side, creates an impressive climax to the journey from the coast.

The 'Abbaye de la Paix' (the name later corrupted to 'Bellapais') was founded in the early period of Lusignan rule, becoming a home first for the Augustinian and later the Norbertine orders. With the benefactions of King Hugh III (d. 1284) and his successors the abbey grew in size and importance up to the time of the Genoese lootings in 1373, when most of the treasures of the church and monastery were removed. The decline of the abbey continued during the Venetian and Turkish periods and it was not until recent years that serious restoration work was undertaken. Unfortunately this has gone hand-in-hand with the commercialisation of the abbey, to the extent that the once charming square to the south has now been deprived of its character by new development.

The abbey should be approached from the west, and entered by an arched **gateway** under a tower that was part of the fortifications, now largely ruined, that were added in the 14th c. Passing through the forecourt the visitor enters the 13th c. **church** which is the earliest surviving part of the abbey. Excluding the iconostasis, which is a Greek Orthodox addition, the interior is of a Frankish Gothic church, with a nave and two aisles, a north and south transept, and a chancel. From the north transept a night stair leads up to the dormitory; to the west a spiral staircase gives access to the roof. Returning to the forecourt, a doorway on the north side leads to the peaceful and enchanting centrepiece of Bellapais, the abbey **cloister**. Although it is a partial ruin the beauty of the cloister is not lost: rather it is enhanced by the delicate if stark outline of the arches of the arcade to the west, deprived of the vault they once supported. The Gothic detail in this cloister is interesting: particularly the carvings on the corbels (heads of animals and humans) and on the bosses at the vault intersections (rosettes, Lusignan coats of arms). In the north-west corner of the cloister is a large marble sarcophagus of the 2nd c. AD, in which the monks used to wash their hands before entering the refectory. Over the refectory entrance, in the north-east corner of the cloister, are three finely-carved coats-of-arms, of Jerusalem and the Lusignans and of the royal quarterings of Cyprus which combine the two. The **refectory** has a fine Gothic interior, unmatched by any other monastic building in Cyprus. Traces of the benches at which the monks sat can be seen against the walls, and at the east end of the refectory, under the rose window, the higher bench suggests the position of the abbot's table. A pulpit from which the scriptures were read during meal times is built out from the north wall. This is reached by a staircase carved out of the thickness of the wall. From the west end of the refectory a door leads to the kitchen and cellarium, which were once adjoining. Other parts of the abbey now largely ruined are the **chapter house** and **undercroft**, on the east side, and the monks' **dormitory** which was once above them. These are best viewed from above, from the roof of the cloister which can be reached by a staircase from the ground level. All that survives of the dormitory is its west wall, with recesses carved in each bay that served as the monks' personal cupboards. In the small square chapter house below, adjoining the ruined undercroft, note the stone benches of the canons, and the playful carvings on the corbels. The last room to be viewed at this level is the vaulted **treasury**, built over the north aisle of the church. The church's fine belfry can also be admired from the roof, and magnificent views of the foothills of the Kyrenia range.

Boghaz A small fishing port and seaside resort with pleasant beaches, 15 m. north of Famagusta.

Buffavento Castle (3,100') is the highest of the three Byzantine castles in the Kyrenia range. It can only be reached on foot, a climb of about ¾ hr. up a steep path that commences at the end of the road 2 m. north of the monastery of Ayios Chrysostomos. The Italian name *Buffavento* (French *Bufevent*) meaning 'blown by the winds' could hardly be more appropriate for this dizzily-perched fortress that appears from below to be part of the rock on which it stands. The original castle, built as part of the island's coastal defences in the 11th c., was first mentioned in history as a refuge for the Byzantine despot Isaac Comnenus, pursued here by Richard the Lionheart in 1191. It was subsequently re-fortified by the Lusignans, who maintained it as a prison stronghold. A garrison remained here until the middle of the Venetian occupation, when the castle was abandoned and dismantled. Today it is very difficult for the visitor to reconstruct the castle visually, partly because it is so ruined and partly because of the steepness of the rocks on which it was built. The layout is rather haphazard, and in the absence of a guide the visitor is advised to follow the demarcated path and stairway.

The ruins A gateway leads to the **gatehouse** of the Lusignan period, and here the ascent begins to the chambers of the **Lower Ward**, one of which is built over a vaulted water system. A further flight of stairs leads to the **Upper Ward** at the highest point of the rock, where there are the remains of a chapel and other buildings. From here the visitor can look down, often through a veil of white cloud, on awesome views of the Kyrenia range and the northern coastline.

Caledonian Falls (4,000') Beauty spot, ½ m. north of Platres, reached by following the old road to Troodos, along the valley of the *Kryos Potamos* stream. Though the stream is perennial, the falls are best seen in the early part of the year, after the winter rains.

Cedar Valley A unique area in the Paphos Forest region on the west side of the Troodos, between Kykko Monastery and the forest station at Stavros tis Psokas. The only surviving natural habitat in Cyprus of the beautiful *cedrus brevifolia*, a cedar unique to Cyprus, which is now a protected tree.

Chrysorroyiatissa Monastery (3,700'), on the western side of the Troodos, is one of the most hospitable — and certainly one of the most finely situated — monasteries in Cyprus. From a spur of land it commands a striking panorama of the Paphos region: a fertile, delicately-terraced valley open to the lower slopes to the west and sealed to the east by a back-drop of sheer-walled mountains. Dedicated to the Holy Virgin, the monas-

Chrysorroyiatissa Monastery

tery was founded in the 12th c. by the monk Ignatius, who after his discovery of a miraculous icon on the seashore was directed to this spot (Mt Royia) by the Virgin. The name of the monastery derives from *chryso* ('golden') and *royia* ('pomegranate'), the combination suggesting an attribute of the Virgin, 'golden-breasted'. The silver-encased icon remains virtually the only relic of the original monastery, which has suffered from decay and successive fires. The present building, which is modern, offers accommodation to visitors.

Coral Bay An attractive bathing spot on the coast north of Paphos with delightful beaches, tinged pink by deposits of finely-crushed coral. The area is now being developed as a holiday village.

Curium (Kourion) One of the ancient Greek settlements founded in Cyprus between the 12th and 14th c. BC, and the most important after Salamis. Situated on the coastline near Episkopi, to the west of Limassol, it lies in an area that prior to colonisation by the Achaean Greeks had been continuously inhabited since the Neolithic period. The Greek city successively accepted the domination of the Assyrians and the Egyptians, but under the Persians became more selective in its alliances. During the rebellion of the Greek hero Onesilos against the Persians (500 BC) Curium joined forces with its sister-city of Salamis; but at the right moment, when the Persians were getting the upper hand, changed sides. Support for the Persians, which was to prove such an embarrassment during their wars against Greece, was finally abandoned in the 4th c. BC, when the King of Curium, Pasicrates, led a Cypriot fleet against the Persians at the siege of Tyre, in support of Alexander the Great. During the Hellenistic and Roman periods Curium remained a prosperous and important city, only to suffer the fate shared by the other great city states in Cyprus: first the ravages of earthquakes in the 4th c. AD and then of Arab pirates in the 7th c. Formerly a centre of the cult of Apollo, Curium became a bishopric during the early period of Christianity. After the final destruction of the city in the 7th c. the seat of the bishop was transferred to Episkopi. The ruins, originally excavated by the Universities of Pennsylvania and Missouri and currently by the Cyprus Department of Antiquities, are extensive.

City centre The access road to the site lies to the south of the main road, partly hidden from the east by a bend at the top of a hill. The custodian's office lies a short distance along this road and cars may be taken through the gate for the drive to the theatre. At this point, however, it is convenient to visit the area of the most recent excavations. To the left (opposite the custodian's office) is the **fountain house**, with some repositioned columns. The main feature of the site is the complex of terracotta pipes which supplied the water from nearby reservoirs. These in turn were supplied by a Roman aqueduct, now vanished, which brought water to the city from mountain springs. Skirting a rise in the ground beyond the fountain house one reaches a group of newly-excavated public buildings (work is not yet completed on the site).

The most interesting complex, to the west, includes a large private house of the late Roman period (3rd–4th c. AD), the **House of the Gladiators**. This house, lying to the east of a newly-excavated section of the city wall, comprises a central courtyard surrounded by a portico and various rooms, including baths. On the floor of the courtyard can be seen the unique mosaics, of gladiatorial combat, which gave the house its name.

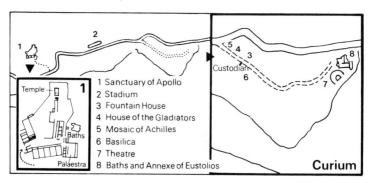

1 Sanctuary of Apollo
2 Stadium
3 Fountain House
4 House of the Gladiators
5 Mosaic of Achilles
6 Basilica
7 Theatre
8 Baths and Annexe of Eustolios

Curium

Another, more prominent, hill lies to the west. On the far side is the building which houses the **Mosaic of Achilles** (4th c. AD). This mosaic, depicting a scene from Greek legend in which Achilles, disguised as a maiden, is unmasked by Odysseus, is part of the pavement of a colonnaded portico, on the north-east side of an open courtyard. The building has other mosaic pavements, in an inferior state of preservation.

Returning to the main entrance gate the visitor will see, on the right, the ruins of an **Early Christian basilica**, probably the cathedral church of the first bishop of Curium. The nave of the church, which is about 100' long, is defined by the bases of the twelve granite columns that separated it from the aisles. In front of the apse, in the chancel, the position of the four columns supporting the baldachino over the altar can also be traced. It is unfortunate that so little remains of this church, which was built after the destructive earthquakes of the 4th c. AD. Its despoliation is certainly the work of man, rather than nature. Following the path towards the sea, the visitor can admire the siting of the ancient city, on a cliff 300' high with a commanding view of the coastline. In the most dominant position, on the very edge of the cliff, is the remarkable **theatre**, a restoration of the Roman building of the 2nd c. AD. This itself replaced an earlier Greek building which was more of a 'theatre in the round' with a circular orchestra enclosed by a horseshoe-shaped auditorium. The Roman plan is semi-circular but with a deeper auditorium, capable of holding an audience of about 3,500. Behind the orchestra can be seen the foundations of the scene-building, which originally reached to the full height of the auditorium. During one period of its history under the Romans the theatre was adapted for wild animal fights; later, however, it was reconverted for use as a theatre. Now, in its restored state, it is regularly used for public performances of music and drama. Immediately to the east of the theatre lie the ruins of the **Baths and Annexe of Eustolios**. This palatial building, dating from the 5th c. AD, was the work of a man called Eustolios, whose name appears in a mosaic in one of the rooms. Designed originally as a rich man's villa, the building was converted to use as a recreational centre, whose main features were an entrance vestibule, garden-court and rooms, all with fine mosaic floors, and a bathing establishment. This is set at a higher level than the rest of the building and is reached by a flight of steps to the north. It includes a central room with mosaics, one of the panels bearing a representation of *Ktisis*, the personification of Building or Creation, who is holding a measure in her right hand. Around the central room are the baths themselves: to the north and east the *frigidaria* (cold baths) to the west the *tepidarium* (warm room) and *caldarium* (hot room).

Stadium The site of the stadium is reached by returning to the main road and continuing west for $\frac{1}{2}$m., beyond the limits of the ancient city. Built in the 2nd c. AD, the stadium was used for athletic contests until 400 AD. Excavations (1939–47) revealed a U-shaped plan with three gateways and seating for 6,000 spectators. Part of this seating, which was in seven rows, has been reconstructed.

Sanctuary of Apollo A mile further along the road, to the west, lie the remains of the sanctuary dedicated to Apollo Hylates ('protector of the forests'). Appropriately set in a grove of pine and cypress trees, these ruins commemorate the god whose cult was the most celebrated in Greek mythology and which made this a sacred spot for 1200 years (800 BC–400 AD). The ruins are of a Roman reconstruction of the sanctuary, following an earthquake in the 1st c. AD. The site should be entered from the west, by the Paphos Gate, and to reach it visitors approaching from the south will pass the remains of a long rectangular building with five separate rooms, whose function was perhaps the pagan equivalent to the hospice, accommodating the visitors to the temple. A similar purpose may have been served by the building to the north-west, reached by a flight of steps. Both buildings were probably also used for the storage of the multitude of votive offerings brought to the temple by worshippers. These objects — mostly the terracotta figures now seen

Mosaic of Ktisis, Curium

in the Kourion (Curium) Museum at Episkopi and elsewhere — had occasionally to be disposed of and it is interesting to note, walking east towards the Curium Gate, a votive pit from which a large collection has been recovered. North of this point lies a paved road, leading to the remains of the **Temple of Apollo**. The altar of the god, which may have been nearby, has disappeared. South of the temple are the remains of a sacred precinct where animals were sacrificed, with buildings further south that have been identified as a priest's house and treasury. Leaving the sanctuary by the Curium Gate, the visitor descends a flight of steps into a colonnaded **palaestra**, used for the training of athletes. In one corner of the central court stands part of a stone water jar which the athletes used for their ablutions. Outside the sanctuary, to the north of the palaestra, are the remains of the **baths**, a complex including dressing rooms, cold-water baths (with mosaic pavements) and hot rooms.

Dhali see **Idalion**

Dhekelia Village 8 m. north-east of Larnaca in Larnaca Bay that has given its name to one of the two British Sovereign Base Areas.

Drepanum, Cape West coast, north of Paphos. The site of a Roman city, not yet fully excavated. There are also the remains here of an early Christian town which for identification has been given the name of **Peyia**, a village 9 m. inland. The ruins include three basilicas and a bath-house. The baptistery of the main basilica has a fine mosaic pavement with scenes from nature reminiscent of Roman mosaic decoration. On a promonotory overlooking the sea is the isolated **Chapel of St George.**

Emba Village 2 m. north of Paphos. The **Church of Panagia Chryseleousa** belongs to the 12th c., with three aisles and two domes. As in many Byzantine churches in Cyprus, the roof is finished with mortar. In 1744 a narthex was added to the church, with an external staircase to the roof. The original decoration of the church has been lost and the later, post-Byzantine work has also deteriorated, much of it obscured by repainting in the 19th c. The church has however a number of important icons from the 16th c., including one of two panels, preserved under glass, of the *Twelve Apostles.*

Enkomi/Alasia Ancient site near Salamis, north of Famagusta. The earliest remains at this site have been dated at 2000–1700 BC, and the city can thus be related to the first historical reference to the island (c. 1500 BC) in which the Egyptian Pharaoh Thotmes III records the receipt of a tribute in copper from 'Asy', an early name for Cyprus. The city was at this time an important trading and copper-exporting centre and is generally thought to have become the capital of the kingdom of Alasia, the name by which Cyprus was later known. In the 11th c. BC, after a disastrous series of earthquakes, the city was abandoned in favour of the new settlement of Salamis on the coast. The first work on the site was carried out by the British in 1896, but up to 1934 the only discoveries were a number of tombs, some containing precious objects, which suggested a rich necropolis for the nearby city of Salamis. Subsequent excavations, under the direction of the French Professor Schaeffer (and with the co-operation of Professor Dikaios of the Cyprus Department of Antiquities), revealed the existence of houses and an enclosing wall defining the area of an ancient city (approx. 1 sq. m.).

To the visitor's eye, the city is very difficult to visualise, for two reasons. First, nothing stands above ground level. Second, the layout of some of the larger buildings is confusing, due to the practice of the inhabitants of dividing them into smaller units at a later date with rubble walls. A guide to the site is essential, and can be obtained from the custodian. The site is still being excavated, and the full history of the city is yet to be revealed. Of the buildings uncovered the most important are, from the south: the **House of the Bronzes**, discovered in 1934, where many fine bronze objects were unearthed; the **House of the Pillar, Building 18**, with an impressive facade of stone blocks; and the **Sanctuary of the Horned God** where one of Cyprus' most prized treasures (the little bronze statue of the horned god now in the Cyprus Museum) was found.

Episkopi Village 9 m. west of Limassol, which owes its name to the transfer here of the Greek Orthodox bishopric from Curium in the 7th c. In the village is the **Kourion Museum**, which houses relics from ancient Curium, 2m. away. The museum is best reached by a turning opposite the *cafenion* at the western entrance to the village (next to the petrol station). A further left turn at the mosque leads uphill past the police station to Museum St (Odhos Museio).

*****Famagusta** The history of Famagusta is comparatively brief, unless one considers it as an extension of the earlier cities of Salamis and Constantia to the north. The refugees from Constantia, which had been destroyed by the Arabs, joined an existing settlement here, but it was not until the arrival of the Christian refugees after the fall of Acre in 1291 that Famagusta began to develop from a small village to a prosperous merchant city. Its natural deep-water harbour, the only one in the island, ensured its growth as a trading centre for the Middle East, the ships bringing in spices, perfumes and ivory and taking out the products of the island – sugar cane, wine and silk. Fortified by the Lusignans, Famagusta was later taken over successively by the Genoese and the Venetians. The present fortifications are those of the Venetians, who valiantly but unsuccessfully defended the city against the Turks in 1571. **The town** Famagusta is no longer one town but two. The old walled city is the joint masterpiece of the Lusignans, who built its churches, and the Venetians who built the present fortifications. The new town, **Varosha**, was largely the product of the tourist boom of the '60s. Since the 1974 Turkish occupation Varosha (originally a purely Greek-Cypriot area) has been maintained as an unoccupied zone pending a settlement.
The walls of the old city are a massive record of the engineering skill of the Venetians, who after taking over the island in 1489 remodelled and reinforced the existing Lusignan walls, turning Famagusta into one of the most impregnable fortified cities in the Middle East. In 1571 the walls withstood the bombardment of the Turkish cannon and catapults during five months of siege, in which no less than 100,000 missiles pounded the city. The walls (average height 50', varying thicknesses up to 27') remain much as they were in the 16th c., with the exception of new openings on the north, south and east sides. A journey round the moat is possible by car or on foot, entering by the Djamboulat Bastion. From here one can see that the moat has been excavated in places out of the rock on which the walls were built.
Walking tour of the old city Starting point: the **Land Gate**. Cars can be parked just inside the Land Gate. The moat is crossed by a 19th c. bridge to a modern entrance. To the left, notice the original gateway. Behind it the huge **Ravelin**, a fortification containing guardrooms and

Sanctuary of Apollo, Curium Above: Land Gate and Ravelin, Famagusta

dungeons. A ramp ascending through a large Gothic arch leads to the top of the Ravelin, one of the best vantage points overlooking the old city. From here it is possible to walk along part of the ramparts on the old sentry walk. Returning to the road follow the wall to the Martinengo Bastion in the north-west corner of the city. On the way note five disused churches. In a street to the right, the **Church of the Nestorians**, built in 1359. Until the recent political separation of the communities it was used by the Greek Cypriots as an Orthodox church. Further along the main road, to the north, is the 14th c. **Church of St Anne**, now locked but with visible frescoes, Next the little **Tanner's Mosque**, originally a Christian church, and the tall, ruined **Church of the Carmelites**, belonging to a monastery of that order which has now disappeared. Nearest the bastion is the small Armenian **Church of St Mary** – also once part of a now extinct

monastery – which was built in 1346. These last four churches, virtually isolated from the modern dwellings of the walled city, present a remarkable glimpse of a medieval corner of Famagusta, much as it must have appeared 600 years ago. The **Martinengo Bastion**, jutting like a spearhead from the north-west corner of the city, was the most impregnable part of the fortifications. Inside, note the beautifully curved walls of the passages connecting the rooms, and the gun embrasures commanding the north and west walls. The main feature of the fortifications is the moated citadel, identified as **Othello's Tower**, that commands the seaward defences of the city. Its name arose from its associations with the 16th c. military governor of Cyprus, Christoforo Moro – the 'Moor' of Shakespeare's play. The original citadel of the Lusignans was a square-towered enclosure with battlements: under the Venetians (1492) the towers were reduced to the level of the

Famagusta Old City Walking tour

1 Land Gate
2 Ravelin
3 Nestorian Ch.
4 St Anne Ch.
5 Tanners Mosque
6 Carmelite Ch.
7 St Mary Gate
8 Martinengo Bastion
9 Othello's Tower
10 St George of the Latins Ch.
11 Sea Gate
12 St Nicholas Cathedral
13 Venetian Palace
14 St Francis Monastery
15 Templars and Hospitallers Ch.
16 St Peter and St Paul Ch.
17 St George of the Greeks Ch.
18 Ayia Zoni Ch.
19 St Nicholas Ch.
20 Djamboulat Bastion

battlements and rounded. This and the strengthening of the walls are typical of the Venetian adaptations to the city's defences, marking the transition from bow-and-arrow to cannon warfare. At the entrance to the citadel the winged lion of St Mark is sculpted in stone above the name of the architect-governor, Nicolo Foscarini. Inside the citadel is an attractive courtyard surrounded by vaulted chambers from the Lusignan period. Some of these, filled in by the Venetians, have not yet been fully excavated. From the ramparts of the citadel, commanding views of the sea and the walled city, one can more readily appreciate its function both as an inner defencework and as the strong point of the harbour defences. Near Othello's Tower rise the lofty ruins of Famagusta's first Gothic church, the **Church of St George of the Latins**, dating from the end of the 13th c. Only the choir and part of the north side of the building remain. The **Sea Gate**, south of Othello's Tower, is now closed. On the right the massive gate is guarded by a 16th c. Venetian lion.

St Nicholas Cathedral (Lala Mustafa Pasha Mosque) Built in the early 14th c. by the Lusignans, this former Latin cathedral, the dominant building in the old city, is a model of the French Gothic architecture of the period. The characteristic features are the beautiful west front, with its gables and triple porch, and the twin towers, of which only the lower parts remain. The Turkish bombardment of 1571 and subsequent earthquakes caused considerable damage to the cathedral (destruction of towers and buttresses) and its original form underwent further modification with its conversion into a mosque. The addition of a minaret and the reorientation of the interior do little however to detract from the overall gracefulness of the structure, and the whitewashing of the interior walls, pillars and ceiling has served to enhance the Gothic line. The fretted Islamic windows have replaced the stained glass of the Latin church, but the impressive rose window in the west front has been retained. Up to the Genoese occupation of the city in 1374 the cathedral saw its greatest period of glory under the Lusignans. In their elaborate coronation ritual each ruler was successively crowned King of Cyprus in the Cathedral of St Sophia in Nicosia and — after a forty mile procession to Famagusta — as King of Jerusalem in St Nicholas.

Outside the cathedral to the south of the parvis or cathedral square stands a Venetian loggia. Opposite, on the far side of the main square, the three arches

(flanked by granite pillars from the ancient city of Salamis) mark the portico that is the only remnant of the **Venetian Governor's Palace**, once occupied by the redoubtable defender of Famagusta, Bragadino. The court behind it was the scene of the Venetian Captain's final submission to the Turks, and his celebrated execution. North of the Venetian Palace are the remains of the 13th c. **Monastery of St Francis**, and opposite, those of the two **Churches of the Templars and Hospitallers**. Of the other Gothic churches of Famagusta, the best preserved is the **Church of St Peter and St Paul**, built in the 14th c. Its transformation into a mosque assured its survival, although it is no longer used for that purpose. On the street leading back to the Sea Wall stands an interesting, and at first perplexing ruin: the **Church of St George of the Greeks**. The wide semi-circular apse, flanked by two smaller apses, contrasts oddly with the Gothic architecture on the north side. This conflict of style came about when the original Greek Orthodox cathedral was adapted by the Lusignans to harmonise with the other architecture of the city. This church was severely damaged in the Turkish bombardment. On the way to the Djamboulat Bastion, at the south-east corner of the city, are two further small Byzantine churches, **Ayia Zoni** and **St Nicholas**. The **Djamboulat Bastion** is the point where the heroic Turkish general Djamboulat Bey died in an attempt to capture the arsenal. His tomb is now within the bastion, which has been converted into a commemorative museum. From the Djamboulat Bastion complete the tour by following the south wall back to the Land Gate.

Overleaf: Fresco in Church of Panagia Podithou, Galata

Above: St Nicholas Cathedral, Famagusta

Galata (2,000') Village in the Troodos region (Solea Valley) with three painted churches. To see them apply to the priest's house north of the village opposite the white-painted roadside church of Ayios Paraskevi.

In the village is the **Church of Ayios Sozomenos**, which like others in the region is covered by a steep-pitched roof, extended over a screen-type enclosure. The paintings, of the early 16th c., are well preserved but obscured by smoke. At the entrance (external north wall) is the *Last Judgement* (left of door) and the *Tree of Jesse* and *Councils of the Church* (right). Inside the church is the New Testament cycle, with some rarely-depicted scenes from the *Life of the Virgin*. Note the *St George* (west end of north wall) and scenes from his martyrdom.

South of the village, in a field to the west of the Troodos highway, stand the other two painted churches. The larger of the two, the **Church of Panagia Podithou**, was built in the early 16th c. by the Venetian Coro family. The paintings in the interior show the Italian Renaissance influence of the period. The style is best seen in the fine *Virgin Mary Enthroned with Christ and Archangels* (apse) and the *Crucifixion* (north pediment). Close to this church is the **Church of the Archangel** or **Panagia Theotokos**. This was once the chapel of the Venetian family of Zacharia, painted by the local artist Simeon Afxendis in 1514. A portrait of the *Donors* (north door) is particularly interesting: note the signature of the artist in the centre. The New Testament cycle is shown in the upper zone of the walls and on the western pediment: on the lower zone the saints. In the apse, the *Virgin Mary and Archangels* (conch) and the *Six Fathers of the Church* (below). The paintings are notable for the freshness of their colours.

Halevga (2,000') Headquarters of the Northern Range Division of the Forest Department. In the centre of the Kyrenia range, east of the Pentadactylos mountain, this makes an ideal stopping place for the traveller journeying from either Kyrenia (22 m.) or Nicosia (15 m.) along the unmade forest road to Antiphonitis Monastery. Refreshments are available.

Idalion Site of ancient city, 15 m. south-east of Nicosia, set in a bare eroded landscape near village of **Dhali**. Two of the hills to the rear of the village served as a twin acropolis for the city kingdom, but they have not yet been fully excavated and there is little for the casual visitor to see.

Kakopetria (2,200') Village in the Troodos region, in Solea Valley 3 m. north of Galata. The village lies on both sides of the valley. To the east is the summer resort, popular with those seeking the coolness of the mountain region but a lower altitude. To the west, across the river, is the old part of Kakopetria, one of the last surviving examples of a typical Cypriot hill village. By the main road, at the south entrance to the village, is the **Church of Panagia Theotokos** (key from petrol station). This church has paintings of the local post-Byzantine revival style (early 16th c.) with a portrayal of the donors over the entrance.

Visitors to Kakopetria will, however, be encouraged to visit the more important **Church of Ayios Nicolaos tis Steyis** (St Nicholas of the Roof) 3 m. outside the village. Like most of the other painted churches this church is locked and application for the key and a guide should be made to the *Kentro* further up the road. Built and decorated in the early 11th c., St Nicholas of the Roof is recognised as the most historic painted Church in Cyprus. It is also the most perfectly sited, on a wooded slope high above a rushing stream. The church is cruciform in shape with a dome and narthex, the whole covered with a steep-pitched roof. These outer roofs, which became common in the area, were a later addition, serving as an extra protection against the snow and rain of the mountains. The paintings inside the church cover an extraordinary span of ecclesiastical art, from the 11th to the 15th c. From the Byzantine period note particularly the double painting of the *Transfiguration* and *Raising of Lazarus* (south side of west vault) and the *Triumphal Entry of Christ into Jerusalem* (north side of west vault). From the late 13th c.—early 14th c. come the *Crucifixion, Anastasis* and *Empty*

Monastery of St John Lampadistis, Kalopanayiotis

Tomb (vault and lunette, north transept) and from the late 14th c. the *Birth of Christ* (south vault). The latter painting shows unusual details: the Virgin suckling the new-born Christ and, at the bottom of the picture, a shepherd playing a bagpipe.

Kalopanayiotis (2,400') Village in the Marathasa Valley in the Troodos, 5 m. north of Prodhromos. In the village, on the east side of the river, is the disused **Monastery of St John Lampadistis** For the key, continue past the west end of the bridge to the priest's house (on the right, after two churches).
The monastery combines several buildings of different periods, the whole covered by a large barn-like structure with a steep-pitched tiled roof. The complex includes: The **Church of St Heracleidius** (11th c.). This domed, cross-in-square church contains frescoes of two periods. From the early 13th c. is the *Christ Pantocrator* (dome) *Ascension* (vault, south transept) and *Entry into Jerusalem* (west vault) and other paintings in the west transept and on the piers, pendentives and drum of the dome. Note also the large *Archangel* on the right of the west door. The remaining paintings in the church are of the late 15th c. The **Church of St John Lampadistis** (originally 12th c.,

rebuilt in 18th c.) was added to that of St Heracleidius after the burial here of St John Lampadistis. The skull of the saint is preserved in a niche over his tomb, by the north-east pier which is the only survival from the early building. In the narthex common to both churches, on the east wall, is a *Last Judgement* of the late 15th c. and portrait of the *Donors.* The **Latin Chapel** is a vaulted building added in the late 15th c. and contains a series of frescoes showing the influence of the Italian Renaissance that resulted from the increasing dominance of the Latin Church in Cyprus. Note particularly the saints in the portraits of the *Twelve Apostles* in the vault. The little entrance door to this chapel is a fine example of 16th c. Cypriot wood-carving.

Kanakaria Church Near the village of **Lythrangomi**, in the Karpas peninsula 33 m. north-east of Famagusta, is the **Church of Panagia Kanakaria** This church, which stands outside the village to the left of the main road approaching from the west, contains the second of the island's two surviving Byzantine mosaics. The church, recently restored, is of different periods. The nave and two aisles are an 11th c. reconstruction of an earlier basilica, whose sole remnant is the central apse containing the mosaic. The domed narthex at the west end of the church was built on to the church in the 12th c. The central raised dome was added in the 18th c. The priest lives adjacent to the church and may be summoned by a bell at the west entrance. The **mosaic** in the conch of the apse, although representing the same subject as that of Kiti (*The Virgin Mary and Child attended by Archangels*) is of a more primitive style and thought to be of the 5th or 6th c. Unfortunately only a fragment of the mosaic survives, but it is enough to make one appreciate the original beauty of the composition.

Kantara Castle (2,000') is the eastern-most of the three castles on the Kyrenia range. It is reached by a second-class road from Trikomo, and although lower in altitude than Buffavento or St Hilarion affords dramatic views of the Karpas or 'panhandle' to the east, the thickly-forested slopes of the Kyrenia range to the west, the Bay of Famagusta to the south and – to the north – a glimpse of the distant mainland of Turkey. Built as the last link in the chain of Byzantine coastal defences, Kantara's first mention in history was as the refuge in 1191 of the despot Comnenus, who later surrendered to the besieging army of Richard the Lionheart. Fortified by the Lusignans, the castle was

Above: Ayios Nicolaos, Kakopetria

dismantled by the Venetians in the 16th c. **The ruins** Although the buildings within the castle were demolished the outer wall is still — after some restoration — impressively intact. The name 'Kantara' (Arabic, meaning 'escarpment') refers to the sheer walls of rock on which the castle was built and which makes it accessible only from the east, where the slope is more gradual. On this side an outer wall provides additional protection and the visitor enters a ruined **barbican**, guarded by twin towers, before climbing the steps to the main entrance of the castle. Opposite the custodian's office, on the left, is the entrance to the **south-east tower**, which contains a large vaulted guardroom and beneath it a cistern, originally used as a prison. The most convenient tour of the castle is in a clockwise direction, starting by the path leading along the south wall. The first building, on the left, was a small **barracks**, and has three rooms pierced by loopholes. At the end of the building is a latrine, flushed by a conduit that was part of the intricate drainage system of the castle. Further on, to the right, are the remains of another cistern, shaped like a horseshoe. Continuing along a demolished section of the fortifications, to the south-west corner of the castle, the visitor will discover five more **chambers**, one of them with a gated opening kept as an emergency exit. Turning north, and continuing past more ruined chambers and cisterns, the visitor will find the path that leads up to the **highest point** in the castle. Here the south wall of a ruined chamber stands, complete with a medieval Gothic window. This tower was used to transmit messages to Buffavento, the next link in the defensive chain. Descending from the summit and continuing on the main path, the visitor will reach the **north-east tower**, which is entered through a passage. The square central chamber of the tower in turn gives on to a narrow projecting fortification, with loopholes on either side, that flanks the entrance to the castle. The tour is completed by returning along the east wall to the main entrance.

****Karpas** The eastern peninsula, or 'panhandle' of Cyprus.

****Kephalovryso** ('head water') Name shared by two mountain springs in the Kyrenia range. The first is the source of the river that runs through Kythrea, northeast of Nicosia, and the second supplies the fertile region of Karavas and Lapithos, west of Kyrenia. The latter spring, which is perennial, issues from a rock (alt. 850') reached by road from Lapithos.

Khirokitia The earliest evidence of human habitation in Cyprus lies in this neolithic settlement (5800 BC), 23 m. east of Limassol. The site is on a small hill, and was chosen for the proximity of the river to the east, and the fertile land to the south. The life of the first settlers — whose origin is unknown — has been revealed in some detail by the discoveries made at the site during the excavations, which began in 1936. Flint sickle blades and the bones of domestic animals provided evidence of early agriculture. From a later period of settlement (c. 3500 BC) fragments of pottery were unearthed, the 'combed' ware that may now be seen, with other relics, in the Cyprus Museum.

Only a small area of the settlement has been excavated, and it will be noted that the foundations of the circular dwellings (*tholoi*) built originally of stones from the river bed, have been strengthened with concrete to retain their original form. Most of the houses were single-roomed, but it is interesting to notice one of them, just inside the entrance, which has two large stone piers rising from the floor. These were used to support a mezzanine. The walls of the huts were made of stones set in mud, and the domed roofs of mud brick, and the work of excavation was greatly complicated by the constant process of rebuilding that these crude dwellings had undergone. As each hut fell into disrepair it was flattened and a new building erected on the site. Over the centuries many building levels were superimposed, and the street — which now, after excavation, resembles a high stone wall — had to be maintained at the same level. Perhaps the most dramatic discoveries at Khirokitia, made by the director of the excavations Dr Dikaios, were the human skeletons found buried in each successive layer, or floor, of the dwellings. The bodies of the deceased, bent double, were placed in shallow pits in the floor, and their belongings buried with them. Successive generations of the same family were buried in one house, and from a single dwelling 26 burials were found in eight superimposed floors.

Kiti Village, 6 m. west of Larnaca, famous for the **Church of Panagia Angeloktistos** ('built by angels') in which may be seen one of the finest mosaics in the Byzantine world. This mosaic, with the apse that it decorates, are thought to be a survival of an early Byzantine church destroyed by an Arab raid in the 7th c. The rest of the church dates from the 11th c., with 14th c. additions, notably the Latin chapel (now serving as a narthex) to the south.

The **mosaic**, depicting the *Virgin Mary and Child attended by Archangels*, is one of the most beautiful interpretations of the subject. The figures are identified by Greek inscriptions. The two Archangels Michael and Gabriel, wearing wings of peacock feathers, each carry an orb and sceptre, symbols of the power of Jesus throughout the world. The ·Virgin Mary ('Hagia Maria') stands on a footstool, bearing the Child in her left arm.

Kition (or Kitium) see **Larnaca**.

Kolossi Castle, 7 m. west of Limassol and close to the main road outside Kolossi village, is the great monument to the Knights of St John of Jerusalem (Knights Hospitallers) who were granted land here by the Lusignan King Hugh I in the early 13th c. For a century this was the home of the Order until it transferred to Rhodes, but up to the time of the Venetian occupation (1489) it remained the headquarters of the Grand Commandery of the Order which controlled 40 villages in the area. These villages, producing wine and sugarcane, ensured the lasting wealth of the Order and the name survives today in the popular dessert wine still produced in the area, *Commandaria*.
Keep The great square keep, with its yellow stone walls and cypress tree sentinel reaching to almost the same height, presents one of the most striking pictures of medieval military architecture in Cyprus. It was built, in fact, in 1450,

after earlier fortifications had suffered damage in Genoese and Mameluke raids. The coat-of-arms of the builder, the Grand Commander Louis de Magnac, is set into the east wall, with other escutcheons. The walls are 9′ thick and the building has three storeys. At the ground level are three storage chambers, originally reached through a trap-door from the floor above. The first floor is the level at which the keep is entered, via a staircase on the south side which has replaced the original drawbridge. Before entering note the machicolations at the level of the battlements, used for pouring oil on anyone attempting to storm the entrance. Inside the keep is an entrance hall with a painting of the *Crucifixion* on the wall to the right of the entrance: below it the fleur-de-lys of the arms of Louis de Magnac. Also at this level is a room containing a large fireplace, probably a kitchen. The second floor, reached by a spiral staircase, contains two further rooms with five fireplaces: the antechamber and apartment of the Grand Commander. Each room has four windows, with seats built into the recesses to the thickness of the walls. The staircase continues to the battlements, which were largely restored in 1933.
Sugar factory and mill To the east of the castle are some interesting ruins. The large vaulted building (south) was used for making sugar from the locally-grown sugar-cane, one of the island's principal exports in the Middle Ages. Next to the sugar factory (north) are the remains of the mill that served it. The medieval aqueduct further north is still used for irrigation.

Kornos Village 23 m. south of Nicosia, 1 m. west of the Limassol road. The local soil — the 'terra nova' — makes excellent pottery clay and has provided the village with an important industry. The pottery, which is worked entirely by hand, is of traditional style and function: storage jars, water and wine vessels.

Kouklia see **Palea Paphos**.

Kourion see **Curium**.

Koutsovendis Village 7 m. north-east of Nicosia on southern side of the Kyrenia range. To the north, on the road leading to St Chrysostomos Monastery, are the remains of a 12th c. **church** with a wall painting of the *Lamentation over the Body of Christ*.

Kykko Monastery (3,800′) situated on the west side of the Troodos, is the island's principal monastery, owing its

foundation and enduring celebrity to the gift of an icon of the Virgin Mary in the 12th c. This is one of the only three such icons in existence attributed to the hand of St Luke. The icon itself cannot be seen, but stands encased by a silver representation of the Virgin in front of the iconostasis of the church. The chandeliers in the nave of the church, gifts from Greece and Russia, indicate the prestige of the monastery, which for many centuries has had a strong influence within the whole Orthodox Church. In the church's treasury can be seen a collection of bishops' crowns, relics and a 12th c. bible. The present buildings of the monastery date from a fire in 1813 and are grouped round two courtyards with cloisters. 70 rooms have been made available for travellers wishing to stay overnight. From a vantage point above the monastery, some of the finest views of the Troodos can be enjoyed. On the highpoint 1½m. above the monastery is the *Tomb of Archbishop Makarios III* and a small shrine.

* **Kyrenia** The origin of this small town and resort on the north coast was in the city-kingdom of Kerynia, founded in the 10th c. BC by the Achaeans. The plentiful water supply from the Kyrenia range and the fertile soil ensured a history of settlement for the area, revealed today by extensive excavations, most notably at Karmi and Lapithos. Like the other ports of Cyprus, threatened first by pirates and then by the Arab invaders, Kyrenia became a walled city with the main defences centred on the harbour. Apart from the castle, greatly fortified in later times by the Venetians, the main relics of these Byzantine defences are four towers. The first of these is situated in the centre of the harbour and was probably used as a lighthouse or a pier to which a chain could be attached to block the entry of vessels in time of war. The other towers, originally linked by walls, are at different points in the town.

The town (pop. 3,500) The central attraction of Kyrenia is its horseshoe-shaped harbour, flanked by the majestic Venetian castle. The best view of the harbour is from the castle, where one can enjoy in a glance the double backdrop of the tall Venetian buildings – so observantly reconstructed – that embrace it and the mauve peaks of the Kyrenia range beyond.

Kykko Monastery

The castle The building that originally occupied this site was the Byzantine fortress in which the wife and daughter of the despot Isaac Comnenus took refuge after the conquest of the island by Richard the Lionheart. The castle was enlarged during the reign of the Lusignan King Hugh I (1205–18) and was used by the Lusignans as a residence and as a retreat in times of war or unrest. The Lusignans' maritime rivals, the Genoese, attacked the castle in 1373, but the walls were never breached. After their seizure of the island in 1489 the Venetians strengthened and modified the castle much in the style of Famagusta. The best examples of their work are the projecting north-west rounded tower (viewed from the harbour, the most prominent feature of the castle) the west wall and the square south-west bastion. For those who have been to Famagusta, the latter fortification will be related to the Martinengo Bastion, with embrasures at three different heights to allow three levels of fire over the south and west moats. The castle is entered by the modern bridge over the dry moat on the west side, which at one time, filled with sea-water, may have provided an inner harbour for the protection of ships in time of war. Through the entrance passage the visitor ascends to the **gate-house**, and from here it is best to explore the castle in a clockwise direction, not going through the gatehouse but turning first to the north-west tower. On the way to the tower is a small **Byzantine chapel**, built into the thickness of the north wall. This has been largely restored, but retains the four ancient columns from the original structure. From the **north-west tower** it is possible to walk along the battlements of the 13th c. north wall and then either continue along the fighting gallery on the east side or descend via several chambers to the courtyard. In a large hall on the east side of the courtyard a remarkable exhibition has been mounted. From a gallery can be seen the remains of the **Kyrenia Ship**, a Greek trading vessel that sank off the coast of Kyrenia in 300 BC. The ship, discovered by the diver Andreas Cariolou, was recovered from a depth of 90′, ¾m. offshore, by a team of archaeologists from Pennsylvania University. The salvage operation took two years (1968–69) and the reconstruction a further six years. This involved soaking the timbers of the hull in a bath of preservative which enabled them to be dried and reassembled to provide a miraculous reconstruction of the oldest ship ever to be recovered from the sea-bed. In an adjacent room is an exhibition of the objects carried on the ship. 2,200 years ago: wine amphora, grain mills, lead weights for fishing nets, cooking and eating utensils. Across the courtyard a staircase leads to the upper storeys of the **west range**, which are thought to have housed the royal apartments of the Lusignans. The only rooms now remaining are a large vaulted chamber on the middle storey and a Latin chapel, now roofless, on the upper storey. Below these upper floors are the dungeons, carved out of the rock, and a small vaulted cell. Ascending to the battlements of the south wall of the castle it is interesting to observe the result of recent excavations, which have cleared much of the rubble used by the Venetians to fill in the space between the outer, Lusignan wall and the inner, Byzantine wall. The latter wall has now been clearly exposed. From the square **south-west bastion** the visitor can walk back along the west wall and descend by a staircase to the entrance.

Lagoudhera (3,000′) Village in the Pitsilia region of the Troodos, approached via the Khandria-Polystipos road by an unmade road (1m.). West of the village is one of the oldest and finest painted churches in Cyprus, the 12th c. **Church of Panagia tou Arakou**, with paintings recently restored by the Dumbarton Oaks Byzantine Institute (Harvard University). The key is available at the adjacent monastery building.

The plan of the church is a single aisle with a vault and central dome, the whole covered by an outer roof and enclosure. Set in the side walls in the position of transepts are two facing recesses. The paintings belong to the main Byzantine period (end of the 12th c.) and relate the Christian story in colourful detail. Supreme in the dome is the *Christ Pantocrator.* Then, in sequence, we have the *Annunciation* (eastern pendentives) *Presentation of the Virgin to the Temple* (lunette of north recess) and *Birth of Christ* (south side of western vault) the latter with a delightful study of the infant Jesus being bathed by attendants. The *Presentation of Christ in the Temple* (wall of north recess) includes an expressive study of St Simeon holding the young Christ. A smaller recess, to the left of the north recess, contains the *Baptism of Christ,* a composition beautifully adapted to its arched surround. The west wall of the church, removed for the addition of the present narthex, is thought to have continued the story with the Passion and Crucifixion. The next surviving composition in the sequence is the *Anastasis* (north side of west vault) with Christ standing on the gates of Hell about to depart with Adam and the saints. Completing the cycle is the fine *Ascension* (eastern vault) and the *Dormition of the Virgin* (lunette of south recess).

Lambousa was the name adopted by the ancient settlement of Lapithos (on the coast, 8 m. west of Kyrenia) during its period of greatest prosperity under the early Christians. Little of interest remains now on the site of the Roman and Byzantine cities, but the name 'Lambousa' ('brilliant') is justified by the treasures recovered from the period when this was a bishopric (61 AD–13th c.). Close to the sea stands the disused **Monastery of Achiropiitos** ('built without hands') with a church that combines the architecture of several periods (12th–16th c.). The rooms of the monastery are used at present by the army, but visitors are permitted. Nearby stands a strange rock-hewn **chapel** from the early Christian period and, nearer the sea, the striking little domed **Church of St Eulalios** (16th c.) named after one of Lambousa's bishops.

Lapithos Village 8½ m. west of Kyrenia, noted for its lovely setting: orange and lemon groves, the gentle northern slope of the Kyrenia range. The evergreen nature of this part of the coastline is due to a perennial stream (Kephalovryso) issuing from the mountainside above the village. It made the area a natural choice for settlement for the Greeks in the 12th c. BC and since then there has always been a population either here or at Lambousa on the coast. In the pre-Roman period Lapithos was one of the minor city-kingdoms of Cyprus: under the Romans it became one of the administrative capitals of the island.

Larnaca (pop. 29,000), a small town and port on the east coast, was in ancient times (as Kition) the great rival to Salamis.
Kition was founded in the 13th c. BC by the Mycenaeans and enjoyed its greatest prosperity under the Phoenicians in the 8th c. BC. As the seaport for the rich copper mines of Tamassos, Kition became a focal point for Levantine trade, and the alliance between the Phoenicians and the Persian rulers of Cyprus ensured its protection. In the war between Greece and Persia, however, Kition was besieged and reduced by the Greek navy under Cimon of Athens (450 BC). This was the beginning of a turbulent period in the city's history. Its continuing allegiance to Persia brought it into violent conflict with Salamis during the revolt of the anti-Persian king of Salamis, Evagoras. After

its renunciation of Persia in 351 BC. Kition became with the whole of Cyprus part of the empire of Alexander the Great, and was involved later in the struggles between his successors during the early Hellenistic period. Kition (or as it was later known, Kitium) remained an important city up to the time of the Arab invasion in the 7th c. AD, when it suffered the destruction shared by the other coastal cities. It did not revive until the Middle Ages when Famagusta, the most important port, fell into the hands of the Genoese and the re-named Larnaca took its place as the port of embarkation for the Crusaders and pilgrims on their way to the Holy Land. Larnaca's most famous native son was Zeno the philosopher, born in 326 BC.

The town Despite its long and dramatic past there is little of interest to the observer of history in this small coastal town. The most attractive part is the sea front, with its palm-lined promenade and friendly coffee shops and bars reminiscent of the Riviera.

Larnaca: Church of St Lazarus

At the northern end is Larnaca's **marina**, run by the Cyprus Tourism Organisation, with berths for 210 yachts. At the southern end stands a Turkish **fort** of 1625.

Pierides Museum This archaeological and folk museum in Zenonos Kitios Street is open daily from 10.00–13.00.

The ancient city Ravaged by the Arabs, most of ancient Kition is now buried under the modern town. Excavations in several areas, however, have uncovered the evidence of her two most important cultures. In 1930 the Swedish Cyprus Expedition explored the acropolis area, recovering Phoenician statues. It was thought at this time that Kition had been founded by the Phoenicians, but then, in 1959, evidence of Mycenaean settlement was revealed in excavations nearby (Area II, the only site open to visitors).

The ancient sites are reached from the marina, via Afxentiou Avenue. At Kimon Street a turning is made to the **Archaeological Museum**, which houses some interesting relics from Kition and local sites. Following Kilkis Street one passes, to the north of the museum, the site of the *acropolis* of Kition, whose excavations have been largely filled in and are not accessible to the public. Crossing Archbishop Kyprianos Avenue into Zakinthos Street, turn left at Makhera Street and again at Pasikrati Street to reach the major site, **Area II**. This is a corner of the northern part of the ancient city, enclosed by the city wall. The earliest remains here are of the 13th c. BC, but superimposed on them are the massive structures of the 12th c. Mycenaean settlement. The most impressive remains of this Late Bronze Age development are the Cyclopean *city walls* and the large *Temple I* which was converted by the Phoenicians in the 9th c. into the even larger *Temple of Astarte*. A detailed guide to the excavations is available from the custodian.

A further Mycenaean site, overlaid by Hellenistic baths, lies at the north end of Kimon Street (not open to visitors).

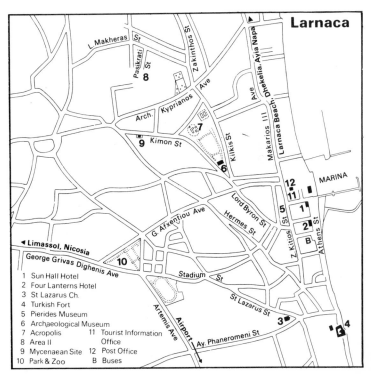

Larnaca

1 Sun Hall Hotel
2 Four Lanterns Hotel
3 St Lazarus Ch.
4 Turkish Fort
5 Pierides Museum
6 Archaeological Museum
7 Acropolis
8 Area II
9 Mycenaean Site
10 Park & Zoo
11 Tourist Information Office
12 Post Office
B Buses

Church of St Lazarus Set in the heart of the market quarter of Larnaca, this is one of the most unusual and appealing churches in Cyprus. Its individuality lies in its white-painted belfry, a remarkable survival in view of the Turkish ban on campaniles, which were feared might be used by the Christian population to signal a rebellion. The church had its foundation in the 9th c., when the remains of St Lazarus, who came to Cyprus after his miraculous resurrection by Christ, were discovered in the town and entombed here. Unhappily the relics were shortly removed to Constantinople and thence to Marseilles, but the empty tomb remains and can be seen beneath the floor of the sanctuary. To recover the church from the Turks after their conquest of the island, the Christian communities bought it back from the invaders in 1589, from which time it was used jointly for Latin and Greek Orthodox worship. Outside, on the wall to the left of the porch, the evidence of this joint use is shown by the funerary inscriptions in Greek, Latin and French. Inside the church, the most interesting features are the three domes over the nave, the rococo pulpit built into one of the pillars and the Royal Doors (1659) at the south entrance with Lusignan and Byzantine coats-of-arms. On the south-east pillar an icon depicts the *Raising of St Lazarus*. The interior, including the fine 18th c. iconostasis, was recently restored following a serious fire in 1970.

Lefkara (2,400') comprises two separate villages: Pano Lefkara and Kato Lefkara. They are situated in the south-eastern foothills of the Troodos 5 m. from the Nicosia—Limassol road. They are renowned as the centre for the beautiful hand-made lace and white needle embroidery which has been a local speciality since the Middle Ages. This embroidery is sold throughout Europe and promises to be a continuing industry, with the skills passed on from mother to daughter. In the summer months the women can be seen working at their embroidery in the narrow little colour-washed alleys of the two villages, and the results of their labours can be admired in the lace merchants' shops. A note of advice, before purchasing any lace or embroidery, is to go to more than one shop, as prices vary considerably. Another speciality of Lefkara is Turkish Delight (*loukoumia*) which is made and wrapped in the shops that sell it. Like the lace it is however made largely for countries abroad, where it is rather expensive, and the opportunity should not be missed — by those with a sweet tooth — of taking some home.

Lefkoniko Small town, 40 m. east of Nicosia, noted for its weaving and embroidery.

Limassol The importance of Limassol, the second largest town in Cyprus (pop. 105,000) lies largely in its port and its association with the island's profitable wine industry. Historically, its period of achievement was very brief. In ancient times it was a small settlement midway between the thriving cities of Amathus and Curium, and did not begin to supplant them until the late Byzantine period. In 1191 it sprang into significance when Richard the Lionheart, having landed at Amathus and engaged in a campaign of conquest of the island, brought his future Queen here for a wedding ceremony in the castle. After his departure the inheritors of his conquest, the Lusignans, developed the town, and it saw further progress under the Knights Templar and the Knights of St John who cultivated the now famous vineyards of the area. Like Larnaca, the port of Limassol benefited from the Genoese capture of Famagusta in 1374. Shortly afterwards, however, the Genoese set fire to the town, an act of destruction that was repeated in a series of raids by the Egyptian Mamelukes in the 15th c. In 1570 the town fell to the Turks, and a final catastrophe — an earthquake in 1584 — reduced it to a near-ruin. It was not until the end of the 19th c., when the arrival of the British assured the re-emergence of the wine industry, that Limassol returned to its former prominence.

The town As a resort, Limassol cannot boast the scenic or historical attractions of Kyrenia or Famagusta, but compensates for this by its liveliness. There is a wide choice of hotels, many of them on the sea front, and the restaurants and cafes offer the contrasts of simplicity and sophistication. The night life is similarly varied, with discotheques springing up by popular demand along the route known as the 'by-pass'. Festivals are another feature of Limassol's gaiety, the most famous being the spring carnival and the September wine festival, which lasts for a fortnight. To see wine-making in progress, apply to the Tourist Information Office, or directly to the Keo or Etco breweries. Among other industries of Limassol are fruit canning, soft drinks and carob-kibbling. After wine the principal exports of Limassol are the fruit and vegetables which come from the extensive plantations west of the town. The port, which is now being developed for deep-water anchorage, will play an increasingly important part in the development of the town.

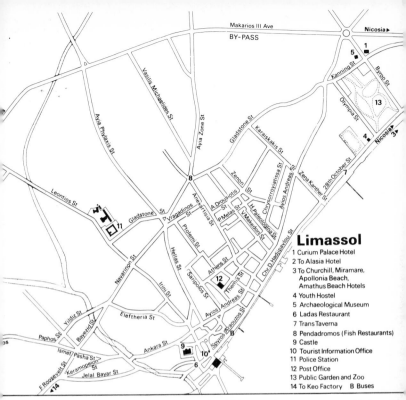

Limassol

1 Curium Palace Hotel
2 To Alasia Hotel
3 To Churchill, Miramare, Apollonia Beach, Amathus Beach Hotels
4 Youth Hostel
5 Archaeological Museum
6 Ladas Restaurant
7 Trans Taverna
8 Pendadromos (Fish Restaurants)
9 Castle
10 Tourist Information Office
11 Police Station
12 Post Office
13 Public Garden and Zoo
14 To Keo Factory   B Buses

The castle Originally Byzantine, Limassol Castle was successively occupied and modified by the Lusignans, the Crusader Knights, the Venetians, the Turks and the British. Within the part that remains is the Great Hall, converted by the Knights of St John into a church but used later as a prison by the Turks and British and a chapel romantically linked to the marriage of Richard I and Berengaria.

Archaeological Museum This new museum houses objects from numerous sites in the Limassol locality, including Amathus and Curium.

Makheras Monastery (2,900'). 26 m. south-west of Nicosia, is situated on the northern slope of Mt Kionia, east of the Troodos range, near the source of the River Pedeios which flows in the winter months from here to Nicosia. The name of the monastery comes from the discovery nearby of a miraculous icon of the Virgin, pierced by a sword (*machaira*). The monks who found it built a church to enshrine the icon, and later, at the end of

the 12th c., a monastery was added. Unfortunately the monastery was entirely destroyed by fire in 1892, and only the icon (now preserved in the modern church) survived. The monastery is however worth a visit for the magnificent scenery it commands: terraced valleys and hills, distant views of the Mesaoria plain. In late February the almond blossom at Makheras provides a vivid spectacle.

*Mesaoria** The large central plain of Cyprus.

*Morphou** Town 24 m. west of Nicosia. Located in the well-irrigated western plain of Cyprus, Morphou is the centre of the main fruit and vegetable producing region of the island. Apart from its citrus plantations Morphou is most famous for its strawberries.
The town should be visited for the monastic **Church of St Mamas**, originally built in the 12th c. over the tomb of a saint who was also a popular hero. St Mamas won the eternal admiration of the Cypriot peasant by his resistance to the

71

oppressive taxation of the Byzantine rulers. The legend has it that when the soldiers came to arrest him he bestrode a savage lion, which he had tamed for the occasion, and rode it to the palace of the prince, whereupon he was granted instant tax exemption! His portrait, astride the lion, can be seen in many village churches in Cyprus, and in this church can be seen the sarcophagus that is believed to contain his remains, built into the north wall so that it is visible from the outside as well. The 12th c. church has been rebuilt several times, but the present structure dates mainly from the 16th c. and shows an interesting combination of Byzantine and Gothic elements. The most impressive feature is the iconostasis, part of which incorporates paintings and carvings from the Venetian period. With the exception of a modern wing (the Bishop of Kyrenia's residence) the monastic buildings are no longer in use.

Moutoullas (2,500') Village in the Marathasa valley, Troodos, between Pedhoulas and Kalopanayiotis. At the highest point of the village is the tiny **Church of Panagia tou Moutoulla**, built in 1280 (key obtainable from the house next to the church). This is the earliest dated example of the typical steep-pitched timber-roof

church of the Troodos region, now covered by a later protective enclosure. The paintings, contemporary to the church, are divided into two series: on the upper wall a shortened cycle from the New Testament (note particularly the *Birth of Christ* and *Crucifixion*), and on the lower wall saints. On the north wall of the apse is a portrait of the donor of the church John Moutoulla, with his wife.

Myrtou Village 17 m. west of Kyrenia, by-passed by the road to Morphou. In the Late Bronze Age **sanctuary**, excavated after the war and recently restored, can be seen a reconstructed altar.

Nicosia The capital of Cyprus, and the only large town not situated on the coast. Its significance, in fact, dates from the Arab raids of the 7th c., which forced the population in some of the exposed coastal areas inland. At this time, after the destruction of Constantia on the east coast, Nicosia became the island's principal city. The modern Greek name of Lefcosia (of which Nicosia is a Latin corruption) has one of two possible origins: the Greek word *lefké* meaning poplar tree, or Lefcon, the name of the founder of the ancient settlement of Ledra on which the city is thought to stand. Nicosia's hey-day, without doubt, was during the time of the Lusignans, when the royal court was established here and many fine palaces and churches built. Its fortifications, however, were not strong and in 1426 the Egyptian Mamelukes sacked the town and seized the king. Cyprus was forced to recognise the suzerainty of the Egyptian sultan, and the king had to pay him tribute. Not until the arrival of the Venetians, in 1489, did Nicosia recover its strength. The city became a military stronghold, with a huge moated wall constructed at some cost to the fine Lusignan buildings. Unfortunately this wall did not prove strong enough to withstand the Turks, who took the city in 1570 after a six-week siege. The population of the city at this time was 50,000; at the end of the Turkish rule three hundred years later it had declined to 11,500. The present population of 125,000 reflects Nicosia's rapid growth in the last century from a drowsy market town to a busy centre of commerce, politics and industry.

The city Like Famagusta, Nicosia is two cities. The difference between the old and the new, however, is not as striking. The Venetian walls of the old city have been reduced in height and penetrated in many places by modern roads and bridges. There is an increasing pressure of new building in the old city, particularly around Ledra street in the Greek quarter. But the contrasts remain. In Evagoras 1st Avenue, running from the complex of Government offices in the new part of the city to Liberty Square at the south-west corner of the old, one might be in any modern commercially-oriented Western city. At the corner of the Bedestan in the Turkish quarter of the old city – particularly on a market day – one might be back in the east of the Ottomans, with ragged street sellers crying their wares and panniered donkeys filing through the narrow streets. These contrasts have been made more apparent today by the physical division of the old city between its two communities,

Nicosia: the old city

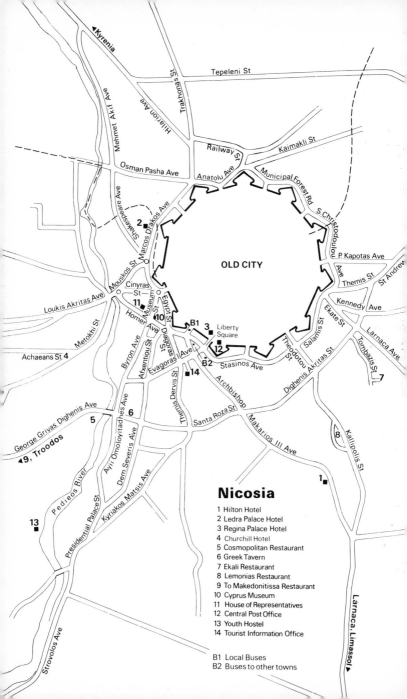

Nicosia

1 Hilton Hotel
2 Ledra Palace Hotel
3 Regina Palace Hotel
4 Churchill Hotel
5 Cosmopolitan Restaurant
6 Greek Tavern
7 Ekali Restaurant
8 Lemonias Restaurant
9 To Makedonitissa Restaurant
10 Cyprus Museum
11 House of Representatives
12 Central Post Office
13 Youth Hostel
14 Tourist Information Office

B1 Local Buses
B2 Buses to other towns

the Turkish-Cypriots in the northern sector and the Greek-Cypriots in the southern sector. With the present restrictions the visitor is obliged to visit the two sectors of the city separately, but it is worth the formalities to see the surviving architecture of the once-proud Crusader city.

The hub of the old and new cities is Liberty Square (formerly Metaxas Square), which is just outside the walls and near the departure points for the inter-town buses. Here one can follow the temptation of the charcoal scents and dine at one of the kebab stalls in the area of the moat – or, with a more sophisticated rendezvous in mind – enjoy an aperitif in one of the café-bars on the adjoining Evagoras or Constantine Palaeologus Avenues. There is no restaurant area in Nicosia like London's Soho, but the choice of tavernas and restaurants with an international cuisine is varied (see map and p. 24).

The **Cyprus Museum** at the corner of Homer Avenue and Museum Street, contains one of the finest archaeological collections in the Middle East. In 14 rooms the visitor can trace the cultural development of the island from the Stone Age to the Roman occupation. The most interesting exhibits are from the earlier periods of history, objects recently excavated from burial chambers in different parts of the island. (Note: following the removal of antiquities from the museum in 1974, some of the rooms are still in process of re-arrangement.)

Room I, devoted to prehistoric Cyprus, has collections from various neolithic and chalcolithic sites. A unique exhibit is a *fresco* from Kalavassos-Tenta (*c.* 5500 BC) showing a figure with upraised arms. This is the only prehistoric wall painting found in Cyprus.

Room II has objects from Early Bronze Age sites (2300–1850 BC). Of special interest are two *clay sculptures* from Vounous which depict in explicit detail a rural scene of two pairs of oxen yoked to a plough, and a sacred enclosure where a sacrifice is about to take place before some priest figures wearing bulls' masks. Also from Vounous is a composite *ritual vase* of red polished ware.

Terracotta figures, Cyprus Museum

From Vasilia is a fine *alabaster bowl* (imported).

Room III is a comprehensive gallery of pottery from all periods of Cypriot history from the Mycenaean to the Hellenistic, including imported ware.

Room IV is devoted to a remarkable collection of terracotta figures, varying in size from a few inches to three or four feet. These are some of two thousand votive objects found round the altar of the sanctuary of Ayia Irini near Morphou Bay in 1929 by the Swedish Cyprus Expedition. They date from the 7th–6th c. BC and represent bull-figures, war chariots, soldiers and centaurs. In *Room V*, a sculpture gallery, is the beautiful marble statue of Aphrodite (1st c. BC) found at Soli. *Room VI*, adjacent, is dominated by the large bronze statue of the Roman Emperor Septimius Severus, found at Kythrea. Also in this room is the delightful small marble figure of a sleeping Eros from the late Hellenistic or early Roman period.

Room VII is in two sections. The first is devoted to bronze objects from the Early Bronze Age onwards. Of special interest is the statuette of a *God Standing on an Ingot* from Enkomi (12th c. BC). From the same period is a *decorative stand* on four wheels, with sides cut out in a design of lions, bulls and griffins. This unusual ornament (there are only two others like it, in museums abroad) was recovered from Germany after

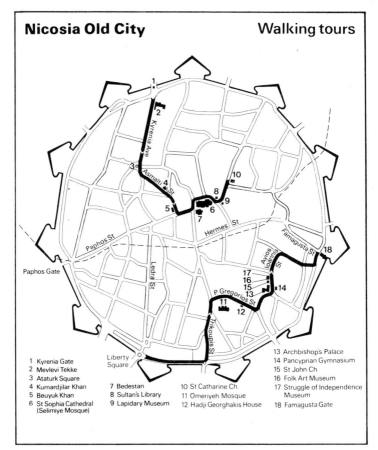

Nicosia Old City   Walking tours

1 Kyrenia Gate
2 Mevlevi Tekke
3 Ataturk Square
4 Kumardjilar Khan
5 Beuyuk Khan
6 St Sophia Cathedral
  (Selimiye Mosque)
7 Bedestan
8 Sultan's Library
9 Lapidary Museum

Liberty Square
Paphos Gate

10 St Catharine Ch.
11 Omeriyeh Mosque
12 Hadji Georghakis House

13 Archbishop's Palace
14 Pancyprian Gymnasium
15 St John Ch.
16 Folk Art Museum
17 Struggle of Independence Museum
18 Famagusta Gate

being smuggled out of Cyprus. *Helmets* of three different styles are from the archaic and classical periods (Kouklia) and the Hellenistic (Athienou). The *Horned God* from Enkomi (see below) also belongs to this section.

The second section of Room VII includes a temporary exhibition of objects, including jewellery, from Palaea Paphos (11th–8th c. BC) and a series of special exhibit cases: Graeco-Roman glassware, early Christian lamps, objects of bone and ivory from the Mycenaean period onwards, and classical and Hellenistic statuettes.

So many of the museum's exhibits were found in tombs that it is interesting to see what some of these tombs were like. In *Room VIII*, in the basement, are reconstructions of six tombs from *c.* 2500 BC to *c.* 400 BC, complete with their contents. In an upper room (*XI*) above the tomb basement are relics from the House of Dionysos at Paphos and from the Tombs of the Kings at Salamis, unearthed in recent excavations.

The gallery leading off Room XI is currently being used for special exhibitions. Among objects displayed here (1981) are the *Horned God* from Enkomi (12th c. BC) and the faience *rhyton* with enamel decoration from Kition (13th c. BC).

Returning downstairs one passes through *Room XIII* (Roman sculpture of the 2nd c. AD) to the final *Room XIV* which has a collection of clay and terracotta figurines from the Early Bronze Age to Roman periods.

The walls of the old city, which are surrounded by a moat and have 11 bastions, were completed in the year of the Turkish invasion, 1570. They withstood a 48-day siege before the city was surrendered to the Turks, who showed little mercy to the Venetian and Cypriot defenders. Built of earth filled with stone, the walls have been greatly altered in the last century, adapted during the British period to meet the demands of modern traffic. The three original gates (named Paphos, Kyrenia and Famagusta after the roads they commanded) are now no longer in use.

The old city Since the 1974 division of the island there has been no access between the two halves of the walled city. Visitors to the *northern sector* must pass through the checkpoint at the Ledra Palace Hotel (for formalities of entering the Turkish sector, see p. 20). They can then walk around the walls to the starting point of their tour, the Kyrenia Gate. (Some points of interest, such as the 14th c. Armenian Church, that are now in the prohibited zone between the two sectors, have been omitted from this tour.)

Kyrenia Gate This gate has suffered

greatly from the development of the modern city. After its closure, openings were made in the walls on either side, turning it into a kind of isolated gatehouse in the middle of the road. Facing the gate is a broad avenue, leading to the heart of the Turkish quarter of the city. To the left of the avenue lies the 17th c. **Mevlevi Tekke**, a former monastery of the Dervish sect. The extraordinary hypnotic dances of this sect were once performed here, and the building now contains a museum of their costumes and musical instruments and an adjacent mausoleum. The avenue opens out eventually into the famous **Ataturk Square**, now dominated by two features: the towering, newly-modernised Saray Hotel and the ancient column in the centre of the roundabout. This was brought to the city from Salamis by the Venetians and originally topped by a lion, the symbol of St Mark. From the square a winding street, Asmalti, leads down towards the centrepiece of medieval Nicosia, the cathedral. On the way, two khans (traditional Turkish inns) are encountered. The first, the **Kumardjilar Khan**, has been restored and is now used as offices. The second, the **Beuyuk Khan**, is now derelict and occupied by workshops. A left turn at the end of Asmalti Street takes the visitor to the cathedral square.

Cathedral of St Sophia (Selimiye Mosque) Here is the most important medieval building in Cyprus: a fine example of the early French Gothic style that even with its twin Turkish minarets strikes an unfamiliar note in this corner of the Eastern Mediterranean. Founded by the Lusignans in 1209, the cathedral was the work of the succession of French craftsmen who followed the Crusades in the 13th c. Some of their finest work can be admired in the porch, with its triple portal and remains of sculptured figures, and in the great west window. Entering the cathedral via the narthex, the visitor should remember that this is now a mosque and that shoes should be removed before going inside. It should also be remembered that formal worship in the Moslem faith occurs five times a day (for 20 minutes) and that although the visitor is allowed into the mosque during these periods he must observe silence. The interior of the building is very beautiful, with a whitewashed Gothic nave flanked by six massive pillars on either side. At the east end, four painted Roman pillars frame the apse. A room to the south, originally used for confession, now contains Christian tombstones prised from the floor of the cathedral at the time of its conversion. On them are carved figures of Frankish knights and their ladies. Though the cathedral has been re-oriented for the Moslem religion (note the prayer platform in the centre of the nave, the mihrab and minbar set into the south transept) the symmetry of the interior is relatively unmarred. The north transept is now reserved for women, who in the Moslem religion are segregated from the men during prayer (note the closed gallery above).

It was in St Sophia that the Lusignan princes were crowned Kings of Cyprus, a ceremony linked, after the fall of Jerusalem, with the second ceremony in the St Nicholas Cathedral in Famagusta, when the newly crowned king was consecrated King of Jerusalem. In the Genoese attacks of 1373 the cathedral was pillaged, and again in 1426 when the Egyptian Mamelukes overran the island. It suffered its final deprivation in 1570 when the Turks, after the capture of the city, removed all Christian ornaments from the cathedral and converted it into a mosque.

Bedestan The beautiful ruined church next to the cathedral was originally the Greek Orthodox cathedral during the Venetian occupation of Cyprus. Its name is the Turkish word for grain store, to which use the church was converted after the conquest. Crossing the narrow street that separates the church from the cathedral, the visitor can admire the beautiful north door with its sculptured frieze and Venetian coats-of-arms above the lintel. Inside, the church is very ruined, with only the north vault intact. From the ground plan of the building it can be seen that it is in fact two churches of different periods, one abutting on to the other. Part of the church houses an interesting collection of medieval tombstones, which may be viewed on application to the attendant of the cathedral.

Behind the cathedral stands the little domed building housing the **Sultan's Library**, a collection of Turkish, Arabic and Persian books founded by Sultan Mahmud II. Near it, the **Lapidary Museum**, an old house devoted to a collection of stone relics from the cathedral and other churches and palaces. To the north, a street leads to the 14th c. **Church of St Catherine**. This church, converted into a mosque after the conquest, has subsequently fallen into disuse. The well-preserved exterior with its warm sandstone walls and finely-carved doors and windows is a delight to the eye, but unhappily the interior is derelict.

The *southern sector* of the old city is best entered from Liberty Square. Running to the north is the main shopping thoroughfare of old Nicosia, Ledra Street. Turning

Inside St Sophia, now the Selimiye Mosque
Below: the Bedestan

right, one follows the wall along Constantine Palaeologus Avenue, past the post office. A left turn at Trikoupis Street brings the visitor to Patriarch Gregorios Street. In an open area on the right stands the **Omeriyeh Mosque**, a former Augustinian monastery where many of the Lusignan nobles were buried (their tombstones are now in the Bedestan).

Further on, on the right, is the oldest house in Nicosia (**No. 18**, the 18th c. house of the dragoman Hadji Georghakis). A left turn at Zeno of Kition Street leads to Archbishop Kyprianos Square, the centre of the Greek Orthodox city. At the southern end is the distinctive, Venetian-style **Archbishop's Palace**, and opposite the **Pancyprian Gymnasium** (High School).

Within the Archbishop's Palace are the **Byzantine Museum and Art Galleries**. The museum contains the island's largest collection of icons, dating from the 9th-18th c.; the art galleries show oil paintings, lithographs and maps.

In the square next to the palace is the restored **Church of St John**, built on the site of a Benedictine abbey in 1665. This is the Orthodox Cathedral of Nicosia, in which the Archbishop of Cyprus is enthroned. The story of the events which led to the establishment of the island's independent (Autocephalous) church is shown in the frescoes on the south wall behind the Archbishop's throne. The scenes show: *The Apostle Barnabas Appearing in a Vision to Archbishop Anthemios; Anthemios Finding the Tomb of the Apostle and Copy of St Matthew's Gospel; Anthemios Presenting the Gospel to the Byzantine Emperor Zeno; Zeno Conferring Imperial Privileges on Anthemios.* (From this time the Archbishop, like the Byzantine emperors, was permitted to wear a cope of imperial purple, carry an imperial sceptre, and sign his name in red ink.)

The church's wall paintings (18th c.) are the only substantial series to be executed in Cyprus since the Turkish conquest. Note particularly the awe-inspiring *Day of Judgement* (south wall).

The next building on the left is the **Folk Art Museum**, housed in a restored 14th c. Benedictine monastery. This contains a comprehensive collection of Cypriot peasant craft, including furniture, tapestry and costumes, and some beautiful church wood-carving. Next door is the **Struggle of Independence Museum**, devoted to the activities of the EOKA movement from 1955-59.

Ayios Ioannis Street leads north out of the square to Theseus Street. A right turn leads back to the walls, and the **Famagusta Gate**, one of the medieval entrances to the city. The entrance has been closed, and unlike the other gates it can be seen virtually in its original form.

Olympus (6,401') in the Troodos range, is the highest mountain in Cyprus. It is reached by road from the Troodos resort (2 m.) and on a clear day gives commanding views of most of the island.

Omodhos (2,500') Village in the Troodos, 7 m. south of Platres. In the heart of the vine-growing region of Troodos, Omodhos is also well-known for its lace-making and for the Festival of the Exaltation of the Holy Cross, which takes place here every year on September 14th. The **Monastery of the Holy Cross**, rebuilt in 1816, contains in its church some interesting relics: the skull of St Philip, given by a Byzantine Emperor, a piece of the True Cross and part of the bonds of Christ, supposed to have been brought to Cyprus by St Helena, mother of Constantine the Great. In the chapter hall of the monastery, now an EOKA museum, note the fine wood carving.

Palekhori (3,000') Village in the Pitsilia region of the Troodos, beautifully situated near the head of the valley of the Peristerona river. At the top of the steep slope on the east side of the village stands the **Church of the Saviour** (tou Soterou) from the 15th c. The key is obtainable from the priest in the village, who will accompany visitors to the church.

The paintings in this church have been attributed to Philip Goul who decorated two others in this region, at Louvaras and Platanistasa. As in the other churches the New Testament scenes are on the upper parts of the walls; the lower parts are reserved for the individual saints. The latter are particularly fine examples of the 15th c. style, reviving the Byzantine tradition; note the *Sts George and Demetrius* (south recess) and the *St Mamas Riding his Lion* (west wall). This representation of St Mamas, who came from Cappadocia in Asia Minor, is peculiar to Cyprus. It pictures him on the lion which he tamed to carry him to the tax-collectors at the Byzantine court. In his left arm he holds his shepherd's crook and the lamb rescued from the jaws of the lion.

Palea Paphos Ancient site adjacent to the village of **Kouklia**, 34 m. west of Limassol. The name 'Palea' or 'Old' Paphos distinguishes this site from that of 'Nea' or 'New' Paphos 9½ m. to the west. Palea Paphos was the ancient Greek settlement, Nea Paphos the later extension of it in Hellenistic and Roman times. This ancient city, sited on a hill overlooking the sea, was capital of one of the earliest kingdoms of Cyprus, and the centre of the cult of Aphrodite until the 4th c. AD, when pagan worship was abolished by the Byzantine emperor Theodosius. In the same century earthquakes destroyed most of the city and little now remains. It is thought, however, that an extensive area of Palea Paphos lies beneath the adjacent village of Kouklia. Evidence for this is in the ruins of the **Temple of Aphrodite** (on the left of the path leading to the custodian's office) which appears to be merely the annexe of a much larger building. The custodian's office is located in the

building south of the excavations known as **La Covocle** (from Latin *cubiculum* meaning 'pavilion'). This was the head-quarters of a royal domain in the time of the Lusignans, administering the local sugar-cane plantations. As at Kolossi there was a sugar factory here. The building now houses an archaeological and epigraphical museum.

Pano Lefkara see **Lefkara**

Pano Platres see **Platres**

Paphos (Ktima) Paphos, 44 m. west of Limassol, is the name that covers the old Graeco-Roman port of Nea Paphos (now known as 'Kato Paphos') and the modern town 1½ m. inland, known as Ktima. Its situation in one of the quieter, more isolated corners of the island might lead the visitor to think of Paphos as an historical backwater. In fact it has a very interesting and dramatic history. Developed round about the 4th c. BC as an alternative to the port of Palea Paphos further to the east, Nea Paphos became a busy port in its own right during the Hellenistic period and eventually replaced Salamis as the capital of the island. Some of its importance was certainly due to its geographical position in relation to Alexandria, and the forests behind it that supplied good timber for ship-building. When the Romans incorporated Cyprus in their eastern province of Cilicia (58 BC)

the island was governed from Paphos by a proconsul. The most famous governor was the orator Cicero, who filled the post for a year in 51–50 BC. A later proconsul was Sergius Paulus who had the distinction of becoming the world's first Christian ruler. He was converted by St Paul, at the end of the apostle's great missionary journey across Cyprus in 45 AD. Subsequently, Nea Paphos became the seat of a bishopric, first in the Orthodox rite and later in the Latin. The first set-back to its pre-eminence came in the 4th c. AD, when the city and port were devastated by the earthquake that created so many of the island's ruins. Constantia (formerly Salamis) became the new capital, and Paphos was further reduced in the 7th c. AD by Arab invasions which continued on and off for a further three centuries. During this period many of the inhabitants of the old city and port moved inland, creating a new settlement. After an attack by the Genoese in 1372 Nea Paphos was finally abandoned and the new town, Ktima, came into being.

Tour of Nea Paphos A car is helpful for this tour, which is quite extensive. Following the road south from Ktima to the port, the visitor approaches the walls of the old city, hewn out of the rock. To the right, just before the entrance, a road leads off to the **Tombs of the Kings**. This ancient site, located in a bare rocky landscape overlooking the sea to the west, was the necropolis of the old city,

Turkish fort, Kato Paphos

and dates from the 3rd c. BC. At this time there were no kings in Cyprus, so it can be assumed that the name of the tombs was suggested by their impressive architecture. There are more than a hundred tombs, scattered round a wide area, and the most striking examples are those that were constructed to emulate the houses, and perhaps the life-style, of the deceased. Around a central underground courtyard, excavated from the rock, is a Doric peristyle, acting as a portico to the entrances of the burial chambers. Each column, and the detailed entablature, has been cut from the rock. The discovery of carved crosses and traces of frescoes in the burial chambers points to their use as catacombs in the early Christian period.

Returning to the main road and entering the old city via the North Gate the visitor will notice a large rocky plateau on the left, known as the **Fabrica Hill**. The rock is honeycombed with chambers, cut out of it in the early Hellenistic period. From the same period (3rd c. BC) are the vestiges of a **theatre**, cut out of the south slope. Further on, two **catacombs** can be visited, on either side of the road. Pagan in origin they were later dedicated to Christian saints. The description 'catacomb' is misleading, as these underground chambers are within the walls and therefore could not have been used for burials. The one on the left of the road is dedicated to *Ayia Solomoni* and includes a chamber converted into a chapel in the 12th c. The

fresco paintings in the apse have been badly damaged by seepage and graffiti, among them the carved names of crusaders. Steps lead down to a holy well. On the right hand side of the road, opposite, is the 'catacomb' of *Ayios Lamprianos*.

Continuing southwards, a column of stone marks the south-west corner and last surviving relic of a **Latin cathedral**, probably built in the 14th c. before the Genoese attack and the retreat of the inhabitants to Ktima. Turning off the main road to the left, along Minoos Street, the visitor will find another survival of the Lusignan period: the domed buildings of some **Frankish baths**. To the south are two churches with legendary associations. The first, to the east, is that of **Panagia Theoskepasti** meaning 'The Holy Virgin Veiled by God'. The name originates from a miracle in the 7th c. AD, when the Arabs were attacking the town and systematically destroying the churches. By an extraordinary phenomenon, the church that originally stood here (as the story goes) escaped the ravages of the Arabs when a cloud descended from the heavens and hid it from sight.

The second church, to the west, is the **Church of Chryssopolitissa**. This church, originally built by the Latins, was later converted to the Greek Orthodox faith during the Turkish period. It stands on the site of an early Christian **basilica**, one of the largest in the island, built in the 4th c. AD and altered in the 6th c. It has five aisles, and

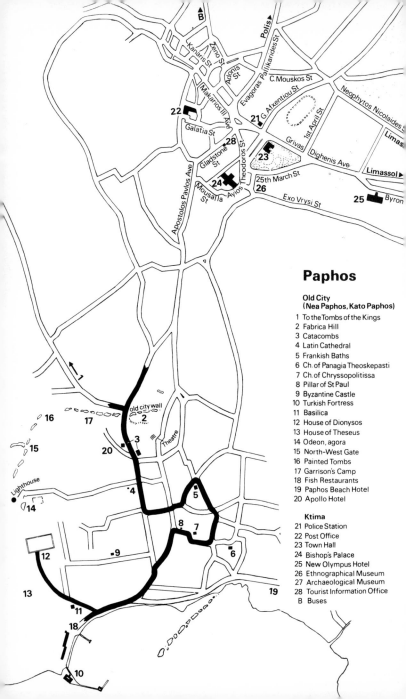

Paphos

Old City
(Nea Paphos, Kato Paphos)

1 To the Tombs of the Kings
2 Fabrica Hill
3 Catacombs
4 Latin Cathedral
5 Frankish Baths
6 Ch. of Panagia Theoskepasti
7 Ch. of Chryssopolitissa
8 Pillar of St Paul
9 Byzantine Castle
10 Turkish Fortress
11 Basilica
12 House of Dionysos
13 House of Theseus
14 Odeon, agora
15 North-West Gate
16 Painted Tombs
17 Garrison's Camp
18 Fish Restaurants
19 Paphos Beach Hotel
20 Apollo Hotel

Ktima

21 Police Station
22 Post Office
23 Town Hall
24 Bishop's Palace
25 New Olympus Hotel
26 Ethnographical Museum
27 Archaeological Museum
28 Tourist Information Office
 B Buses

at the eastern end of the nave, between the central apse and the church of Chryssopolitissa, stand four granite columns which supported part of the roof. The floors are finely paved with polychrome mosaics. The narthex of the basilica lies to the west, partly obscured by the road.

Also to the west, on the other side of the road, are the ruins of a 13th c. Gothic *church* with three aisles, and further on, in the corner of the enclosure, the famous **Pillar of St Paul**, to which the apostle is believed to have been bound and given 39 lashes for preaching Christianity. Much of the material in this area is Roman, and it is tempting to imagine that one is looking at the site of the palace of Sergius Paulus, the Roman governor who converted Paul to Christianity. Turning back to the main road and continuing to the harbour, a **Byzantine castle** 'Saranda Colones' can be observed on a mound to the right, with a reconstructed arched entrance. This was built to protect the harbour from Arab invaders, but was destroyed by an earthquake in 1222. The modern harbour is protected by a small, square **Turkish fort**, built in 1592 over the original Lusignan defences, which had been dismantled by the Venetians in 1570 at the time of the Turkish invasion. The sandstone blocks from the old defences were also used for the long breakwater that curves round the west side of the harbour. Although there is little activity now in the harbour, the quay and the breakwater provide a pleasant stroll. Leaving the quay, and turning inland behind the row of restaurants and coffee-shops, the visitor will discover the ruins of an early Christian **basilica** of the 5th c. AD. He then approaches the climax of the tour of the old city.

Since their accidental discovery in 1962, the **Roman mosaics** of Nea Paphos have become one of Cyprus' greatest attractions from the pre-Christian age. The excavations that followed in the wake of the ploughshare unearthed an extensive Roman villa (c. 3rd c. AD) the **House of Dionysos**, with mosaic floors in an almost perfect state of preservation. The mosaics bordering the *atrium* provide the best examples: on three sides dramatic hunting scenes and on the fourth a mythological series, starting with *Pyramus and Thisbe* and ending with *Apollo and Daphne*. In the largest room, to the west of the atrium, are the remnants of a huge mosaic pavement celebrating the god whose name was given to the house, *Dionysos*. The main panel depicts a vintage scene, and at the eastern end the god is shown riding in triumph in his chariot drawn by two monsters, and attended by his followers. The other pavements have mainly geometric designs, but there are also

figurative mosaics of *Hippolytos and Phaedra, Ganymede and the Eagle, The Four Seasons* and *Narcissus*.

Further excavations to the south conducted by the Polish mission have revealed another, later palace, thought to be the residence of the Roman governor. This takes its name, the **House of Theseus**, from the circular mosaic representing *Theseus Slaying the Minotaur* in one of the rooms on the east side of the atrium. Another fine mosaic, of the *Birth of Achilles*, has been uncovered on the south side. Excavations continue.

The tour may be continued north to the *acropolis* of Nea Paphos, the location of the lighthouse. Below it to the west is a restored **Odeon** (2nd c. AD). In the vicinity are further ruins of the same period, the peristyle court and shops of the *agora* and (to the south of the Odeon) a complex of buildings associated with an *Asklepeion*. Excavations continue on both sites.

The tour may be completed at this point by returning to the main road from the lighthouse. Alternatively, those interested in exploring the rather difficult terrain around the northern part of the ancient city walls may follow the route described below.

Beyond the lighthouse on the north side of the acropolis lies the most prominent part of the **city wall**. This section owes its preservation to the fact that it was cut from the rock, all masonry having been removed. The *North-West Gate* can be identified by a stone ramp, about 120' in length which slopes up to it. The gate was flanked by towers, and at either side of the opening at the top of the ramp are post-holes, used for the support of the gate.

Continuing north around the next angle in the wall one discovers, cut into the exterior of the wall, some Hellenistic **painted tombs**. Off the antechamber lie the recesses for the individual sarcophagi, some with *arcosolia*. The faces of the *arcosolia*, and the walls and ceiling of the antechamber were painted with various patterns, traces of which remain.

Shortly before the north wall joins the road a rocky eminence conceals an elaborate system of rock-cut chambers known as the *Garrison's Camp* (4th c. BC). A vaulted passage has a series of chambers leading off it, some connected by rock-cut steps. It is thought that this was either a sanctuary or, as the name suggests, quarters for the city garrison.

Ktima (pop. 11,000) the small modern town to the north of the ancient port, has a pleasantly relaxed atmosphere, due mainly to its limited commercial and industrial development. Situated on a plateau 500' above sea level, the town offers many refreshing views of the cultivated stretch of coastal plain separating it from the sea, and the delightful distant prospect of the harbour with its tiny yellow fortress.

Archaeological Museum Situated on Dighenis Avenue, this museum has a fine collection of pottery from the Early Bronze Age to the Classical period, marble figures from the Roman city and many relics from the newly excavated House of Dionysos and House of Theseus.

Ethnographical Museum To the south of the town (Exo Vrysi Street) this private museum is open daily. The collection is kept in the traditional house of Mr George Eliades, who will conduct visitors around his remarkable collection of folk art, farm implements, hand-carved furniture, etc.

Paralimni Village on south-east cape, 4 m. north of Ayia Napa, 28 m. east of Larnaca. The coastline on the east of Cape Greco, formerly overlooked, is now being developed. The small cove-like bays offer sheltered alternatives for swimming if windy conditions occur at Ayia Napa. *Fig Tree Bay*, with restaurants, is a 10-minute drive from Paralimni.

Pedhoulas (3,600') Village at the head of the Marathasa Valley in the Troodos, famous for its cherries and spring blossom. In the lower part of the village is the **Church of the Archangel Michael** (key from infants' school near church). This little chapel was painted in 1474 and the work is similar to that of the churches in the Pitsilia region (post-Byzantine local revival). The smallness of the church has restricted the number of scenes from the New Testament to thirteen: note particularly the *Betrayal of Christ* (west wall). Over the north door is an interesting painting of the donor of the church, the priest Basil Chamades, with his family, showing details of contemporary costume. The iconostasis is from the Lusignan period.

Pentadactylos (2,429') is the most spectacular mountain in the Kyrenia range, and owes its name ('five fingers') to its unusual shape, which legend proposes as the handprint of the Greek hero, Dighenis. Pentadactylos may be approached by the forest road, via Halevga or Klepini, and scaled on foot, by the more energetic, via the north face.

Perakhorio Village 11 m. south of Nicosia on Limassol road. At the top of the slope to the west of the village stands one of the most attractive small painted churches of Cyprus, the **Church of the Twelve Apostles** (key obtainable from priest in village). It has a single aisle and a central dome and dates from the end of the 12th c., the closing period of Byzantine rule. The frescoes inside, from the same period, were discovered under layers of cement and whitewash and painstakingly restored by the American Centre of Byzantine Studies. They represent in the dome, *Christ Pantocrator surrounded by Angels*, in the apse the *Virgin Mary with St Peter and St Paul* and below, the *Communion of the Apostles*. Some of the *sinopia*, or under-drawings of the frescoes, have also been revealed.

Peristerona Village 17 m. west of Nicosia on the Peristerona River and at the junction of the main road to Troodos. On the west bank of the river stands the **Church of Sts Barnabas and Hilarion** (key obtainable from café next to church), built between the 10th and 11th c. Its architecture is unusual in Cyprus, being the only church (with the exception of St Paraskevi at Yeroskipos) to have five domes. These are arranged as a cross: three along the nave and one over each of the side aisles. This was a new development in Cypriot architecture, introduced

during the revival of church building in the island after the devastation of the Arab invasions. A further development from the earlier Christian basilicas is found inside the church; the aisles being separated from the nave by arches rather than columns. The narthex at the west end of the church is a later addition. Little survives of the original decoration of the church, now whitewashed, with the exception of a painting on the north-west central pier, from the 16th c. The most interesting features, all from the 16th c., are the iconostasis, an icon of the *Presentation of Christ in the Temple*, some fine painted door shutters, and a wooden chest, in the narthex, used for storing church records, which is painted with a scene of medieval siege.

On the doors of the west entrance, note the elaborate Byzantine wood carving. Worth a visit, if time allows, is the small

Petra tou Romiou, Aphrodite's Bay
Above: Peristerona Church

Chapel of St Barbara, to the south-west of the village, with wall paintings of the 16th c.

***Petra tou Limniti** Rocky island off the north-west coast in Morphou Bay, near the ancient palace of Vouni, fabled as the rock cast by the hero Dighenis on the ships of the Arab marauders. In 1930 evidence of Neolithic settlement was found on the island.

Petra tou Romiou Scenic group of rocks in a bay on the south-west coast, midway between Limassol and Paphos, celebrated in legend as the birthplace of the goddess of love Aphrodite. In another legend the rocks are supposed to have been hurled by the same Dighenis — scourge of the Saracens — who had been similarly engaged in other parts of the island.

Peyia see **Drepanum**

Phassouri plantations, south-west of Limassol, represent the largest acreage of citrus cultivation in the island. Some of the farms may be visited, on application to the Limassol Tourist Information Office. Motorists travelling to Kolossi from Limassol are recommended to take the road via Phassouri (exit road sign-posted Zakaki) to enable them to enjoy the pleasant, tree-shaded roads.

Pitsilia Region of the Troodos, east of Mt. Olympus, popular for its mountain scenery and rustic villages. These villages can be visited on a circular tour, starting either at Khandria to the west or Palekhori to the east. Diversions should be made (time and weather conditions permitting) along the unmade subsidiary roads to the churches of Lagoudhera and Platanistasa, which have Byzantine frescoes. The region is also famous for its vineyards, and it is here (south of Agros resort) that the dessert wine *Commandaria* is produced.

Platanistasa (3,000') Village in the Pitsilia region of the Troodos. 2 m. north of the village on the road to Peristerona, a left turning leads to the **Church of Stavros tou Ayiasmati** (Holy Cross of Ayiasmati) after three miles of unmade road. Visitors should go first to the

village and ask for a guide, who will accompany them with a key. One of a group of three churches in the Pitsilia region (the others are at Louvaras and Palekhori) painted in the post-Byzantine local revival style by Philip Goul, this church has the most complete cycle of wall paintings in the island from this period (late 15th c.). The cycle has 30 compositions: note particularly the *Baptism of Christ* and the *Presentation of the Virgin Mary to the Temple*, both on the south wall of the nave.

Platres (Pano Platres) (3,700') Largest hill resort in the Troodos, with a wide range of excellent hotels and villas and facilities for recreation. It is the focal point for the most scenic walking and riding country in Cyprus, and its altitude (2000' less than the sportsmen's resort at Troodos) makes it popular as a retreat from the heat of the coastal regions during the summer months. A perennial stream (*Kryos Potamos* or 'cold river'), flowing through the village, supplies a natural bathing pool. The Platres Festival, held each year in September, is a great attraction for those interested in the culture of the people of the Troodos region.

Polis Town in western Cyprus, situated 1 m. from Khrysokhou Bay and near the site of the important ancient city of Marion, founded by the Athenians in the 7th c. BC. The latter city was destroyed in 312 BC during the wars between the Alexandrian generals Ptolemy and Antigonus for the possession of the island. A new city was later built on the site of the present town and named Arsinoe, after the sister of the Ptolemaic ruler of the time. The Lusignans, however, came to refer to it simply as *Polis* or 'City'. Although there was a large-scale excavation of tombs from the 4th–6th c. BC (Attic ware, Cyprus Museum) little now remains of the ancient city.

Prodhromos (4,600') Highest village in Cyprus and, after Troodos, the highest resort, offering superb views of the south-western slopes of the Troodos. The former **Monastery of Trikoukkia** (rebuilt in 1761) has now been converted into a research station for fruit-growing.

Pyrga Village 1 m. east of Nicosia-Limassol road, 19 m. south-east of Nicosia. On a slope overlooking the village square is the diminutive **Chapel of St Catherine**, founded by the Lusignan King Janus in 1412. It is perhaps the simplest ecclesiastical building in Cyprus, with a plain, barrel-vaulted interior

Prodhromos

Chapel of St Catherine, Pyrga

decorated with vestigial paintings showing the Italian influence of the period. Note the *Crucifixion* (east wall) with portraits of King Janus and Queen Charlotte at the foot of the Cross and the *Raising of Lazarus* (north-east of vault).

*Rizokarpaso** Town in the Karpas, with a white-painted modern church (**Ayios Synesios**) occupying the site of a former cathedral of the Greek Orthodox Church. This belonged to the See of Famagusta, whose bishop was banished to Rizokarpaso by the Latins in the 13th c.
3 m. north of Rizokarpaso lies the site of the ancient city of Karpasia, destroyed by the Saracens in 802 AD. This was a flourishing Christian community, and it is thought that a remnant of the old city survives in the walls of the ruined church of **Ayios Philon** which stands at the end of the road close to the seashore. Excavations have revealed the existence of an earlier church to the south, with a beautiful marble pavement in geometric style. It is tempting to think of this earlier church as the cathedral of Philon, the 5th c. bishop who converted the people of the Karpas to Christianity.

*St Barnabas Monastery** (Apostolos Varnavas) Near Salamis, 1 m. east of the road junction on the Famagusta road. The present building dates from 1756,

but the original was built in the 5th c. AD after the discovery in a nearby cave of the remains of St Barnabas. This discovery was the most important event in the history of the Cypriot Church, establishing once and for all its independence from the mother church in Constantinople. Barnabas, as well as being the apostle who with St Paul had brought Christianity to Cyprus, was a native of the island: the evidence of his remains, presented by Archbishop Anthemios of Constantia to the Byzantine Emperor, was enough to obtain sanction for the foundation of the Autocephalous Greek Orthodox Church of Cyprus. The Emperor also granted funds for the building of a monastery, on the spot where the saint's body had been found. Unhappily this monastery was destroyed by the Saracen raiders at the same time that they sacked Constantia. The modern **church**, traditional in style, contains little of interest but reflects strongly the personality of the three brother monks whose icons and frescoes — painted by their own hands — adorn it. The three brothers, who have lived in the monastery since 1917, are still engaged in painting icons, which are sold to local churches to provide funds for the upkeep of the monastery. To the east of the monastery stands a small **mausoleum**, covering the rock tomb, now empty, that is thought to have contained the remains of St Barnabas.

*St Hilarion Castle** (2.300') 7 m. from Kyrenia, this is the westernmost of the three castles built by the Byzantines as part of their coastal defences. It is named after a monastery that once stood on the site, originally the dwelling-place of a hermit called Hilarion who fled to Cyprus during the Arab invasion of the Holy Land. Like Buffavento and Kantara Castles, St Hilarion was surrendered to Richard the Lionheart and Guy de Lusignan by Isaac Comnenus, the last Byzantine ruler of Cyprus, in 1191. Re-fortified by the Lusignans, the castle became the focal point of a dramatic trial of strength between contestants for the regency of the island, during the minority of the boy-king Henry I. Possession of the castle — and control of the island — alternated between the legitimate regent, John d'Ibelin, and the arch-claimant, the Holy Roman Emperor Frederick II, several times in a period of four years. The struggle was only resolved by the young king himself, who on returning from a trip to Syria, defeated Frederick's forces at Aghirda, south of St Hilarion. 140 years of peace followed, during which the Lusignan kings lavished money on the improvement of the castle, adding splendid apartments that were to serve as the summer residence of the Royal Family. In 1373, however, the castle was again used for military purposes when the Genoese — at that time attempting to wrest control of the island from the Lusignans — laid siege to it. The defender was another regent: John, Prince of Antioch. A grisly story is told of this siege, which one cannot help recalling when one ascends to the dizzy heights of the castle. The Prince, suspecting the treachery of his Bulgarian guard, had them thrown, one by one, from the castle walls, a sheer drop of several hundred feet. The castle's spectacular history ended with the arrival of the Venetians in 1489. No longer defensible against the more advanced weapons of warfare, the castle was dismantled. It remains, however, the best preserved of the three castles of the Kyrenia range, and repays a leisurely visit. It is divided into three main areas:

Lower Ward This is entered through a double gateway on the south side of the castle, by the visitors' car park. Inside the outer gate, note the **gatehouse**, and to the left of the main entrance, a **barbican**. At the present time the castle is occupied by the Turkish Army and the visitor will be conducted around it by the custodian attached to the garrison. The lower level of the castle was devoted to the quartering of soldiers and horses. To the left, by the south wall, is a **cistern**; further on, to the right, a building used by the Lusignans as a **stables**. The ascent to the next level of the castle offers striking views of the **walls** to the south and west, with their semi-circular towers. These walls, though much restored, are largely Byzantine. The **Middle Ward** is reached through a second **gatehouse**, via a vaulted passage constructed by the Lusignans. On the right, at the top of the steps, is a **Byzantine church**, possibly a survival from the earlier monastery that was used as a royal chapel by the Lusignans. Originally a domed building, with eight supporting arches, the interior has been partially restored, the arches on the east reconstructed to prevent the collapse of that side of the church. To the north of the church, steps lead to a passage adjacent to a large **hall**, a refectory in the monastery which became a banqueting chamber in the castle. The passage leads on to a **belvedere** with a vaulted loggia, with views to the east. Next to the belvedere, and east of the hall, is the **kitchen block** (with chimneys still visible) which belongs to the Lusignan period. The northeast corner of the castle is reached via a passage under the kitchen, and here can

be seen the **royal apartments** and **barrack-rooms**. On this side of the castle a modern restaurant and terrace have been built: a good moment to pause and take in the superb view of the coastline of Kyrenia.

Upper Ward Access to the Upper Ward is at present restricted. It is reached by a steep climb (passing, on the right, an enormous open reservoir) to the highest part of the castle. The area includes service buildings and further royal apartments, the latter containing the graceful **Queen's window**, with its tracery and bench seats intact. A further climb takes the visitor to the highest rampart at the **summit** of the castle, from which the whole layout can be better appreciated. At the centre of the castle rises the isolated **Tower of Prince John** (access also restricted) from which the hapless Bulgarians were flung to their fate.

*Salamis Ancient city kingdom, $5\frac{1}{2}$ m. north of Famagusta. The most important archaeological site in Cyprus, and a 'must' for any visitor to the island seeking a comprehensive view of the history of her civilization. The date of the city's foundation has not been clearly fixed, but recent tomb excavations have revealed artefacts of the 11th c. BC, which would seem to relate the birth of Salamis to the abandonment of the earlier city-kingdom of Enkomi, 2 m. inland. It would also bear out the legend of Teucer, son of the king of the island of Salamis in Greece, who is popularly believed to have founded a settlement on this site after taking part in the Trojan war. Whatever the controversy surrounding its foundation, there can be no doubt that the origins of Salamis are Greek, and that it stoutly defended its position as a Greek city-state against the incursions of the Mediterranean powers. A clay tablet recording a tribute paid to the Assyrian Emperor by the King of Salamis in the 7th c. BC is evidence of a period of Assyrian domination; but throughout this period, and the later Egyptian take-over, Salamis maintained its status as the supreme city kingdom of Cyprus, responsible to the foreign overlord only for the payment of tribute. In the 5th c. BC, however, when the Persians were the main power, there was more militant opposition, first from the hero Onesilos and later from the King of Salamis, Evagoras. Evagoras' struggle against the Persians brought him almost complete control of the island. But after the end of the Graeco-Persian war the Persians reasserted themselves and Evagoras was forced to withdraw to Salamis. After a period of siege the city fell to the

Persians in 380 BC and Evagoras was subsequently assassinated. Persian rule continued until 322 BC, when Alexander the Great's victory at the Siege of Tyre put an end to the Persian Empire. Cyprus then came under the control of the Ptolemies, and Salamis became the centre of a drawn-out conflict between rival generals. One of the most famous sieges in the history of the island was that in which Ptolemy's military governor Menelaus unsuccessfully defended the city against Demetrius, son of Ptolemy's arch-rival Antigonus. During the rule of the Ptolemies, and the subsequent period of Roman colonisation (58 BC—395 AD)

Salamis lost its place as the chief city of the island to Paphos: but its strategic location, on the accessible eastern coast, ensured its continuing importance as a port and commercial centre. In the 4th c. AD Salamis was devastated by earthquakes and tidal waves. The new city, built by the Byzantine Emperor Constantius II took the name of **Constantia**. During the Byzantine period it became once more the capital of the island, and was only abandoned in the 7th c. AD after a succession of earthquakes and Arab raids. Excavations, which commenced in 1890, continue to the present day.

Tour of the ruins The ruins of Salamis are extensive and a car is necessary for a visitor with limited time who wishes to have a general view of the excavations. At the height of the summer extensive exploration on foot can be exhausting, and in such conditions the visitor is advised to allow plenty of time — preferably a day — for the tour, giving himself time off to relax on the beach (which is, incidentally, one of the finest in Cyprus).

The excavations are divided into two areas by the main road from Famagusta. The entrance on the east side of the road leads to the site of the ancient city: but before embarking on the main tour of Salamis the visitor should turn to the west, along the road to St Barnabas Monastery, to visit the **necropolis**.

This begins, on the left, with the **Tomb** or **Prison of St Catherine** (identified by archaeologists as Tomb 50). This isolated building, which has mystified travellers for centuries, has only recently been excavated. The main structure, built of huge blocks of stone, is of the Roman period. Its function at this time is not clear, but the identification with St Catherine, an early Christian martyr, would suggest its later use as a chapel. The excavations carried out in 1965 showed that the building was in fact superimposed on a complex of tombs of the same period as the other tombs in the necropolis (7th c. BC). Skeletons of two yoked horses — now preserved on the site in the ancient entrance passage — were found, with fragments of pottery.

Tombs of the Kings Further along the road to St Barnabas Monastery is the entrance to the area of the royal necropolis of Salamis, with tombs from the 8th–7th c. BC (a custodian will conduct visitors to the more important tombs). These tombs, excavated in 1962, must be counted among the most important archaeological discoveries in Cyprus in recent years. They consist of a funerary

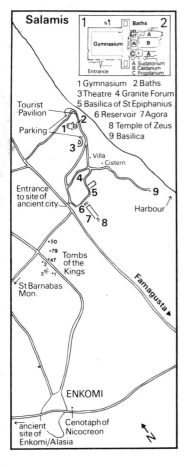

1 Gymnasium 2 Baths
3 Theatre 4 Granite Forum
5 Basilica of St Epiphanius
6 Reservoir 7 Agora
8 Temple of Zeus
9 Basilica

chamber, which contained at one time the remains of a king or members of his family, and a *dromos*, or broad entrance passage, which served as a burial place for the possessions of the deceased. In addition to pottery and objects of ivory and precious metal, chariots were found, complete with the horse teams that pulled them. After the cremation of the deceased, which took place in the *dromos*, the horses which had drawn the hearse were sacrificed. The most interesting tombs are Nos. **47** and **79**, both of which contain skeletons of horses preserved in the cement floor of the *dromos*. Additionally, in Tomb 79, are the remains of four chariots, two of them with horses yoked and with the metal bits of their harness still intact.

The most exciting of recent finds in the royal necropolis of Salamis was the **Cenotaph of Nicocreon**, excavated in 1965/6 by the Cyprus Department of Antiquities under Dr V. Karageorghis. This lies to the south-west of the necropolis, in the village of Enkomi. It consisted of a stone platform built for a funeral pyre, the whole being later covered by an earthen mound, or tumulus. The platform, exposed in the excavations, had four rows of steps and a ramp going up to it. In the bed of the pyre various objects were found which give some idea of the ritual of a royal cremation: gold ornaments, gilded clay bottles, and life-size clay statues. The statues, which were thought to represent members of the royal family, suggest that the funeral might have been purely symbolic (no human remains were found) and the dating of the structure (late 4th c. BC) has related it to the tragic death of the last king of Salamis, Nicocreon, and his family, who committed suicide after the Ptolemaic conquest of the island. The site at Enkomi is of limited interest to the casual sightseer, being largely a reconstruction.

Ancient city The entrance to the ancient city of Salamis is to the right of the main road from Famagusta, and north of the turning to St Barnabas. A guide to the site, published by the Cyprus Department of Antiquities, may be obtained from the custodian. The excavations, which lie between the road and the sea, cover a considerable area: ½ m. from east to west, 1 m. from north to south. Nothing remains of the Greek period and the ruins are of the Hellenistic, Roman and Byzantine periods.

Salamis showing the Baths (left) and Gymnasium with the Theatre in the background

There are three distinct sites: to the north, the Gymnasium, Baths and Theatre; to the south the more scattered ruins of the later Byzantine city of Constantia, with the Roman Agora and Temple of Zeus; to the east, overlooking the ancient harbour, the newest excavations which have uncovered more of the Byzantine city.

Beyond the entrance, near the point where the road forks, can be seen part of the **walls** of Constantia, which if followed on foot will give the visitor an idea of the perimeter of the smaller city that was built in the 4th c. AD to replace the devastated Salamis. The western section of this wall follows the line of the much longer wall of the ancient city. Nothing now remains of this ancient wall except the long banks of earth which indicate its position.

The left fork of the entrance road leads to the tourist pavilion. The visitor wishing to cover the excavations on foot may park here. If on the other hand he prefers to use a car to save time he should leave it at the second car park, between the Gymnasium and the Theatre. The remains in this area are as follows:

Gymnasium This building, perhaps the most outstanding monument to Cyprus'

ancient civilization, was not discovered until 1882, and not fully excavated until 1952. Originally a gymnasium of both the Hellenistic and Roman periods, it later became part of the public baths of the Byzantine city. The colonnaded fore-court, used as a meeting-place in the Byzantine period, was the *palaestra* of the Roman Gymnasium, where the athletes used to train. The columns of the porticoes (most of them cut out of single pieces of marble) are not from the original Roman Gymnasium (destroyed in the earthquake) but were transferred here from the ruins of the Theatre as part of the Byzantine re-construction. The columns were re-erected between 1952–55. The Gymnasium should be entered by the **south portico**. Opposite the south colonnade are two isolated columns which mark the original entrance to the Gymnasium. This entrance was in the form of a triple opening, divided by the columns. The **east portico** adjacent to the front wall of the baths, has a beautiful pavement of coloured marble, with inscriptions, laid when the Gymnasium was reconstructed. In this portico stood a Roman altar, now in the Famagusta Museum, and a number of pagan statues. At either end of this portico are **annexes**, containing rectangular swimming pools. In the north annexe are some of the statues from the Roman period found during the excavations (other examples are in the Cyprus Museum). At the south-west corner of the Gymnasium are the largest ancient **latrines** in Cyprus (semi-circular, with seating for 44 persons).

Baths This building is largely of the Byzantine period, with an impressive facade 12′ thick that at the central point almost retains its original height. Behind it lies the **west hall** of the building, with the hypocaust exposed beneath its collapsed pavement. This was a *sudatorium*, or hot air room, in contrast to the small **bath-houses** on either side with their octagonal tanks, which were *frigidaria* (cold baths). Extending from the west hall is the **main building** of the baths which has a reconstructed east end in the form of an apse. This was a hot water bath or *caldarium*. To the north of it are a **stoker's room** with a floor below ground level to contain the furnace, and a large **north hall** with an apsidal east end and walls of 14′ thickness. To the south of the main building is the **south hall**. Air ducts in the floors of these two halls show that they were used as *sudatoria*. They share another feature: the vaulted recesses (walled up later on to strengthen the building against earthquakes) which used to contain individual baths. Parts of

Roman mosaics which decorated these recesses have been restored to their position.

Theatre To the south of the Gymnasium lies the Roman Theatre, largely reconstructed. Built at the end of the 1st c. BC it was destroyed by the earthquakes of the 4th c. AD. Much of the ruined structure was then removed to provide materials for the rebuilding of the Gymnasium, which had suffered the same fate. The original seating capacity of the theatre (the largest in Cyprus) was about 15,000, accommodated in 50 rows of seats. The excavations, which started in 1960, revealed only eight remaining rows and the auditorium was subsequently built up as part of the restoration of the theatre for classical performances.

To the west of the theatre are further baths of the Roman period, but these are of little interest to the casual visitor, being covered by undergrowth and largely unexcavated. The same is true of much of the area to the south of the theatre, which has a desolate air recalling the seismic disaster that overcame the city that once stood here. Many of the ruins in this area can easily be overlooked: to the left of the road, a **Roman villa**, to the right, beyond the crossroads, the **Granite Forum**, which owes its name to the massive granite columns, some 18′ long, that lie about the site. It is almost possible, too, to miss the most important relic of the Early Christian Church in Cyprus – the **Basilica of St Epiphanius**. So devastated that only its foundations remain, this church (4th c. AD), still conveys an impression of vastness. Measuring 190′ in length by 140′ in width it is the largest ancient basilica in the island and served in its time as the metropolitan church of Constantia. It consisted of a central nave divided by columns from two aisles on either side. The central apse had a semi-circular flight of steps leading up to it, and on either side of it smaller apses built into the thickness of the east wall. Next to one of these small apses, in the south-east corner of the church, is a marble tomb that originally contained the remains of the Bishop of Constantia, Epiphanius, who built the church. After the Arab raids in the 7th c., which left the church a shattered ruin, the returning Christians decided to concentrate their efforts on rebuilding one part of it, to the east of the tomb. This part, which had been an annexe to the old basilica, was converted into a church with a triple dome, which continued in use until the 14th c. South of the basilica are interesting relics from the Roman and Byzantine cities: the **Vuota** or water cistern, built in the 7th c.

AD to receive water carried by the aqueduct from Kythrea; the huge **Roman Agora**, 750′ long by 180′ wide; and beyond it, the **Temple of Zeus**. Of the two latter constructions little now remains: in the Agora lie the broken columns of the porticoes – one on either side – through which the shops were entered: in the Temple of Zeus can be seen the high podium.

Returning to the crossroads, the visitor wishing to see the **Roman harbour** should turn right in the direction of the sea. On the left, in about a hundred yards, he will pass a **Byzantine cistern** which contains, in one of its chambers, inscriptions and paintings (access on application to the custodian). The road leads, eventually, to an area of new excavations. These have been in progress since 1964, the work of a French expedition from Lyons University under the direction of Prof. Pouilloux. The most important discovery has been a **basilica**, from the 4th c. AD. From this point it is possible to go down to the beach, to the site of the now submerged Roman harbour, where it is still possible to find, washed up or buried among the pebbles, shards of pottery made 2000 years ago.

Salt Lake The larger of Cyprus' two salt lakes is at Akrotiri. The smaller, but better-known lake is 3 m. south-west of Larnaca. By this salt lake stands the Turkish shrine the Tekke of Umm Haram. The lake, which is 10′ below sea level, has provided the Cypriots with a natural industry: salt-gathering.* In the summer months, when the water evaporates from the lake, it exposes deep layers of salt, which are gathered into huge pyramids for collection. This lake, like the one at Akrotiri, is frequented in the winter months by a great variety of bird migrants, including flamingoes.

Sanctuary of Apollo see **Curium**

Soli Ancient site in the Morphou Bay, 11 m. west of Morphou. The original city-kingdom of the Greeks, founded in the 6th c. BC, has now disappeared, and only the theatre, which has been largely reconstructed, remains. The city of Soli played a large part in the struggle against the Persians and reached its zenith under the Romans. It was here that the beautiful Aphrodite of Soli, now in the Cyprus Museum, was found.

To reach the **theatre**, approaching from the east, the visitor must take the road junction on the left after leaving Karavostassi (the site of the ancient port). The theatre, carved out of a hillside overlooking the sea, was built in the 2nd c. AD. Discovered by the Swedish Expedition of 1930 it had to be largely restored as little remained after the stone pillaging of the previous century (many stones from the theatre were used in the making of the Suez Canal). The auditorium is mainly new, the entrance passages have been reconstructed, and only the cement and pebble floor of the orchestra and the platform of the stage buildings are original.

Sotira Prehistoric site 5 m. north-west of Episkopi. There is little to be seen here, but the site is worth a visit for those interested in archaeology. The discovery of pottery of the Combed Ware type has related this settlement to the Neolithic II period of c. 3500BC, and the architecture of the houses, of which a few walls have been excavated and reconstructed, shows the difference between this culture and that of the earlier settlement of Khirokitia (5800 BC). A square-walled house has replaced the *tholos* and the floors are not layered. Unlike Khirokitia, the dead were not buried in the houses but in a separate cemetery.

Sourp Margar Monastery (Armenian Monastery) 1 m. from Halevga, to the right of the road from Halevga to Klepini in the Kyrenia range. A modern building including fragments of medieval architecture, long associated with the Armenian Church. Although there are no longer any monks or priests here, arrangements may be made for accommodation with the resident guardian. The location of the monastery, on the wooded northern slope of the Kyrenia range, provides a restful and refreshing pause for the traveller.

Stavros tis Psokas (2,500′) Forest station in the western Troodos, west of Kykko Monastery. Headquarters of the Paphos Forest District, this station administers 258 sq. m. of forest, or two-thirds of the total growth in the island. This area is the only natural habitat of the moufflon, or wild sheep, whose numbers have been greatly reduced over the years by poaching. It is estimated that there are now only 300 of these animals in the wild. In the moufflon enclosure, built in an attempt to conserve the species, a small herd is maintained. Accommodation is available at the forest station (maximum three nights) by application to the Forestry Department in Nicosia.

Stavrovouni Monastery (2,200′) 24 m. south of Nicosia. After Kykko, probably the most visited monastery in Cyprus, famous for its unusual history and unique site. In its history there is an element of legend, for it was here that St Helena, the mother of Constantine the Great, is supposed to have brought the relic of the True Cross from Jerusalem, which brought about the foundation of the monastery.
Its site is spectacular, the summit of an isolated, rock-capped mountain (*Stavro-*

vouni, 'mountain of the cross'). On the way the visitor will pass the **Monastery of Ayia Varvara** with its beehives and vineyards. Motorists should be warned that the ascent to the summit is very steep and the earth road should be treated with caution, particularly in wet weather. Overnight accommodation is offered at the monastery, but not for women. The guardians of the monastery are three monks, whose tour of duty is a month, working in rotation with their brother monks at Ayia Varvara. Their only companions are their cats, which thrive in great numbers. Originally brought in to control the snakes in the area, they now look for alternative sustenance – usually the visitor's picnic. The present buildings of the monastery are of the 17th c. and are remarkable mainly for their fortress-like position on the mountain-top. The views from the terrace, of most of the south-east corner of Cyprus, are magnificent. Inside the church is a beautiful 15th c. wooden crucifix, framed in silver, which is believed to have set into it a fragment of the True Cross brought to the island by St Helena.

Tamassos Ancient site, near village of Politiko, 14 m. south of Nicosia. An early settlement which came into prominence after the discovery of copper (2500 BC), Tamassos is undoubtedly the 'Temese' mentioned in Homer's Odyssey, where Athene went 'in quest of copper'. Its importance can be further attested by the discovery of a number of treasures in the area, identified with various temples of pagan worship. The most interesting discoveries, in 1894, were two **royal tombs**, so called because of their impressive architecture and their date (6th c. BC) which relates to the period when Tamassos was one of the city-kingdoms of Cyprus. The most interesting feature of these tombs is the delicate carving of the masonry, particularly at the entrances. Note the finely-engraved columns, in semi-relief, with their voluted capitals, on the lintel supports. Unfortunately these tombs were looted, and the hole through which the robbers entered can be seen in the roof of the inner chamber of the larger of the two tombs. It is thought that there must be further tombs in this area, and one can only imagine what may one day be revealed when an unpillaged tomb is found. On a hill to the south of the excavations is the **Monastery of St Heracleidius** (rebuilt 18th c.), with a tiny domed chapel held sacred as the shrine of the saint. It was St Heracleidius who conducted St Paul and St Barnabas to Tamassos during their missionary journey across Cyprus. He was ordained by them the first Bishop of Tamassos, and was later martyred. It is believed that his original burial place was below the floor of the chapel. In the church of the monas-

tery are a number of reliquaries — one containing the skull of the saint — and sarcophagi. The monastery has now become a convent and one of its most pleasing features is its garden, carefully tended by the nuns. A local confection, which may be purchased here, is *gliki amigdalou* (almond honey).

Tekke of Umm Haram (Hala Sultan Tekke) Moslem shrine 3 m. west of Larnaca, on the west side of the salt lake. The Tekke (holy place) is the third most important place of pilgrimage in the Moslem world, containing the tomb of a female relative of Mohammed who is recognised as his foster-mother (Arabic *Umm Haram*, Turkish *Hala Sultan* meaning 'respected mother'). This lady, accompanying an Arab invasion of the island in the 7th c., fell from her horse and broke her neck. Her burial place, in the spot by the salt lake where she fell, was marked by three giant stones (two uprights and a horizontal) which are now enclosed in a domed structure inside a mosque. The mosque is situated in a pleasant garden, planted with cypress and palm. Viewed from across the dry salt lake in the summer months, the shrine gives the impression of an oasis.

*** Trikomo** Village at crossroads 13 m. north of Famagusta, on the road to Kantara. In the middle of the central

square is the quaint little **Chapel of St James** (15th c.) which incorporates an unusual decorative feature: porcelain plates inset in its vaulting. The Nicosia road, to the west, leads to the more important **Church of Panagia Theotokos**. This church was built in the 12th c., with a dome and single aisle: the north aisle and western extension being later additions. Little survives of the original wall paintings, which are executed in the rather mannered style of the late Byzantine period. In the dome is a *Christ Pantocrator*, surrounded by angels: in the vault of the apse an *Ascension*. Other paintings of the 12th c., in the arch of the south recess, are remnants of the story of the *Birth of Jesus*. The *Virgin Mary* in the apse is a 15th c. repainting. Of the *Ascension* painted in the vault of the north aisle (15th c.) only the figure of Christ remains.

Troodhitissa Monastery (4,600') 5 m. north-west of Pano Platres in the Troodos. On the west flank of Mt Olympus, and looking out, from the cleft of a river valley, on the forested slopes below, this monastery has a special significance in the Greek Orthodox Church, for here, in the church, is the icon of the Virgin Mary (*Troodhitissa* 'Holy Virgin of Troodos') which was brought here by a monk in the 8th c., during the iconoclastic period of the Byzantine Empire. The monk, wishing to protect the icon from destruction, hid with it in a cave. After his death others continued to guard it until the time came that it could be enshrined in a church. Once a year, on August 15th (The Assumption) Greek Orthodox pilgrims assemble here to celebrate the salvation of the icon. The present buildings are of the 17th and 18th c.

Troodos The central mountain range of Cyprus, with Mt Olympus (6,401') as its highest point. The Troodos region, with its refreshing climate and scenery, is easily reached from Nicosia or Limassol.

Troodos (5,500') Mountain resort, the highest in Cyprus. In the period of British rule this was the seat of government in the hot summer months, and it continues to serve as a refuge for summer visitors from the heat of the plain. It is also popular during the winter months, as a centre for skiing and other winter sports. There are a number of hotels, and good camping facilities.

Varosha see **Famagusta**

Tekke of Umm Haram and Salt Lake

*Vouni Ancient site 14 m. west of Morphou, on a prominent point overlooking Morphou Bay (right fork after Soli, and ascent to summit). The **Palace of Vouni** ('mountain peak') was built in the early 5th c. BC, at about the time of the revolt by King Onesilos of Salamis against the Persians. Although there is no clear record of events it is assumed that the palace was built by a pro-Persian king, after the revolt had been crushed, to dominate the city of Soli, which had sided with the rebels. Later on, in about the middle of the 5th c. BC, a second revolt established a pro-Greek dynasty, which remained here for about 70 years until c. 380 BC, when the Persians regained control of the island. At this time the palace was burnt and destroyed, so it would appear that it existed on this site for little more than 100 years. Excavations were carried out by a Swedish Expedition in 1928–29.

The ruins A conducted tour is essential for this site, and a custodian is available to take parties round at intervals. The walls can only be seen in outline, the lowest levels having been reset in position with concrete: but although so little remains of the palace it has been established that there were four different periods of building. The most important of these occurred with the arrival of the Greeks.

The **apartments** of the pro-Persian king, which had been built in an oriental manner, were converted into a megaron — in the style of the Mycenaean palace architecture. The entrance, changed from the south side of the building to the north, opened on to a **court** at a lower level. The steps to this court, which extend along the full width of the apartments, are still in existence. In the centre of the court was a large cistern, and the stone stele re-erected over the well-head was used to support a windlass. A study of the layout of the drainage channels will give visitors an idea of the sophistication of the water system of the palace, which ensured a readily circulating supply through the main rooms. All round the court are the private rooms of the palace, and, to the east, the **bath rooms**. The construction of these rooms is very interesting, and can be closely related to that of the Roman baths built centuries later. A *caldarium* in which the bathers used hot water adjoins a *frigidarium* in which they used cold water. The floors of these rooms slope down to outlet channels which carried the water to the next room, the *sudatorium* (sweat room) where it was heated by furnaces. The remaining rooms of the palace include store rooms, kitchen quarters and living rooms. A clear idea of their layout can be obtained from the plan in the official guide to the palace, available at the custodian's office. Outside the area of the palace there are a number of pagan shrines, of obscure dedication. At the highest point of the hill, however, lie the remains of the **Temple of Athena**, identified by the sculptures discovered during the Swedish excavations. Among these sculptures were the delightful bronze cow and relief of two lions attacking a bull, now in the Cyprus Museum.

Yeroskipos Village 2 m. east of Paphos, whose name derives from the Greek *hieros kipos* or 'sacred garden', a rest-place in ancient times for worshippers travelling from the old harbour at Nea Paphos to the Temple of Aphrodite at Palea Paphos. The village now owes its fame to two attractions: its *loukoumia* (Turkish Delight) and its church.

The 11th c. **Church of St Paraskevi**, in the middle of the village, shares with the Byzantine church of Peristerona the unusual feature of five domes, arranged in the shape of a cross over a nave and two aisles. The church contains wall paintings from the late 15th c., poorly preserved, and icons from the same period. Of particular interest is the two-sided icon, portraying on one side the *Virgin and Child* and on the other the *Crucifixion*.

Folk Art Museum A short distance from the main square, this interesting collection of peasant crafts, furniture and costume is exhibited in the House of Hadjismith. There are fine examples of carved and painted wooden chests, from Akanthou. Hours: Mon–Fri 0.7.30–14.00, Sat 07.30–13.00. Sun closed.

Yeroskipos Church

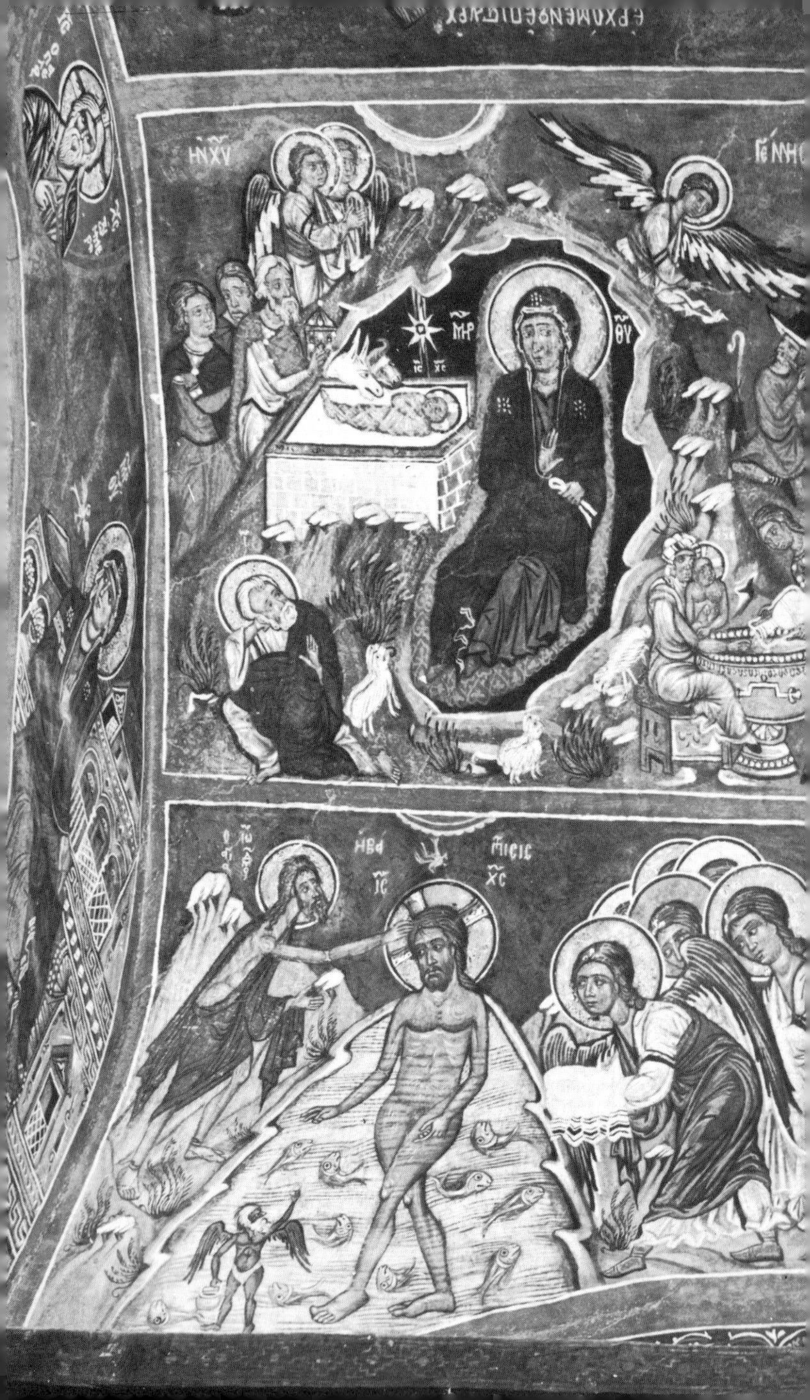